Benjamin Adams Hathaway

1001 Questions and Answers on General History

Benjamin Adams Hathaway

1001 Questions and Answers on General History

ISBN/EAN: 9783741187643

Manufactured in Europe, USA, Canada, Australia, Japa

Cover: Foto ©ninafisch / pixelio.de

Manufactured and distributed by brebook publishing software (www.brebook.com)

Benjamin Adams Hathaway

1001 Questions and Answers on General History

Benjamin Adams Hathaway

1001 Questions and Answers on General History

QUESTIONS AND ANSWERS

ON

GENERAL HISTORY.

REVISED EDITION.

THE BURROWS BROTHERS COMPANY,

CLEVELAND, OHIO.

COPYRIGHT, 1888,

B. A. HATHAWAY.

COPYRIGHT, 1895,

THE BURROWS BROTHERS CO.

CONTENTS.

Egypt,

China,

Japan,

Babylonia,

Persia and Palestine,

Greece,

Rome,

Saracen Empire,

England,

France,

Germany,

EGYPT.

1. *What is History?*
   A record of past events or a record of the rise and fall of civilization.
2. *What is General History?*
   A history of all Nations and Peoples.
3. *Into how many Divisions may General History be divided?*
   Three.
4. *What are they?*
   Ancient, Mediæval, and Modern.
5. *What is the Period of Ancient History?*
   From remote antiquity to the Fall of the Roman Empire, 476 A. D.
6. *What are the limits of the Mediæval Division?*
   From 476 A. D. to the close of the 15th century.
7. *What are the limits of the Modern Period?*
   From the beginning of the year 1500 to the present time.
8. *What is Biography?*
   The history of a single individual.
9. *What is an Autobiography?*
   The history of an individual which has been written by himself.
10. *What is the Derivation of the word History?*
    From two Greek words, which originally meant "To know by inquiry."
11. *What is Political History?*
    The history of States and Empires.

12. *What is Ecclesiastical History?*
    The history of the Christian Church.
13. *What is meant by Sacred History?*
    The historical part of the Scriptures.
14. *What is Profane History?*
    Any history written by uninspired writers.
15. *How many sources have we of historical information?*
    Three.
16. *What are they?*
    Records, Monuments, and Legends.
17. *What People have left their history entirely in Monuments?*
    The Mound-builders.
18. *With what does the History of a people begin?*
    With the formation of settled communities.
19. *What is the Historic Race?*
    The Caucasian, the others having done little worth recording.
20. *How is it divided?*
    Into three great branches: the Aryan, the Semitic, and the Hamitic.
21. *To which one do we belong?*
    The Aryan.
22. *What does the Aryan include?*
    The Persians, the Hindoos, and nearly all the European nations.
23. *For what has it always been noted?*
    Its intellectual vigor.
24. *What does the Semitic branch embrace?*
    The Assyrians, the Hebrews, the Phœnicians and the Arabs.
25. *What has been its great characteristic?*
    Religious fervor.

26. *What has it given to the world?*
The three faiths which teach the worship of one God.
27. *What are they?*
The Jewish, Christian and Mohammedan.
28. *What does the Hamitic branch include?*
The Chaldeans and the Egyptians.
29. *What has it been remarkable for?*
Its massive architecture.
30. *What country is supposed to have been the birthplace of mankind?*
Asia.
31. *What nation had made progress in civilization in a time back of all history?*
The Aryans.
32. *What does the word mean?*
Those who go straight or upward.
33. *What is known of their civilization?*
They dwelt in houses, plowed the soil, ground their grain in mills, rode in vehicles, worked certain metals, calculated up to 100 and had family ties, a government and a religion.
34. *Where does history begin?*
On the banks of the Nile, the Tigris and the Euphrates.
35. *What reason is given for this?*
The rich alluvial soil, the genial climate and the abundant natural products of the earth offered every inducement to a nomadic people to settle and begin a national life.
36. *What are the earliest cities of the world?*
Memphis, Thebes, Nineveh and Babylon.
37. *What is the earliest account we have of Egypt?*
About 2700 B. C., Menes, the half-mythical founder of the nation, is said to have built Memphis, which he made his capital.

38. *Describe Egypt.*
    A flat valley, 2 to 10 miles wide, skirted by low, rocky hills; on the west, the desert; on the east, a mountainous region rich in quarries, extending to the Red Sea. Through this narrow valley the Nile runs for 600 miles.
39. *What is Egypt sometimes called?*
    The "Gift of the Nile."
40. *Why so called?*
    The Nile inundates Egypt every year and then recedes, leaving a deposit of mud which fertilizes the soil to such an extent that two crops are annually raised.
41. *What other advantage is the river to Egypt?*
    It is a means of rapid and ready communication between the remotest parts of the country.
42. *How was Egypt divided?*
    Into several States, but finally was united into two parts: Upper and Lower Egypt.
43. *Name the three Periods of Egyptian History previous to the Persian Conquest.*
    The Old Empire, the Second Empire, and the New Empire.
44. *What is the date of the Old Empire?*
    From remote antiquity to 2080 B. C.
45. *What is the most interesting epoch of the Old Empire?*
    The IVth or Pyramid dynasty, so called because its chief monarch built the three great pyramids at Ghizeh.
46. *Who was the best known of these kings?*
    Khufu, called Cheops (Ke'ops) by Herodotus.
47. *What is a Dynasty?*
    A succession of sovereigns of the same race ruling a particular country.
48. *What may be said of the progress of Arts in Egypt?*
    The useful arts made rapid progress under the Pyramidic Dynasties.

49. *Where did they get their Copper?*
    From the Peninsula of Sinai.
50. *What is the date of the Second Empire?*
    From 2080 B. C. to 1525 B. C.
51. *What famous works were accomplished in the Second Empire?*
    The Labyrinth and Lake Mœris.
52. *What was the Labyrinth?*
    A magnificent group of palaces containing 3,000 rooms, half of them under ground, built as a tomb for kings and sacred crocodiles.
53. *What was Lake Mœris?*
    A gigantic reservoir built to divert the waters of the Nile during an inundation and hold them for the use of the neighboring lands in time of drought.
54. *Who were the first to invade Egypt?*
    Tribes from Asia under the Shepherd Kings.
55. *Who were they?*
    The Hyksos, a rude, barbarian race, who overran the whole region and ruled it for 400 years.
56. *When did Abraham visit Egypt?*
    During the reign of the Shepherd Kings.
57. *What was the date of the New Empire?*
    From 1525 B. C. to 525 B. C.
58. *What is said of this epoch?*
    During this period, there was a national life of 1,000 years which exalted Egypt to the height of its glory.
59. *What great temple was built at this time?*
    The Great Temple of Karnak, now one of the most wonderful ruins of the world. It was connected with the Temple of Luxor by an avenue of sphinxes two miles long.
60. *What was the capital of the New Empire?*
    Thebes.

61. *Who was the greatest monarch of Egypt?*
    Rameses II.
62. *What was he called in Sacred History?*
    Pharaoh, the oppressor of the Israelites.
63. *What did he do for Egypt?*
    He covered the land with magnificent works of art and carried the Egyptian arms in triumph into Asia.
64. *What was the employment of captives who were brought to Egypt?*
    Working in the mines and making brick.
65. *What cruel act was Rameses guilty of?*
    He ordered the Hebrew boys to be thrown into the Nile.
66. *What Ruler was visited by the Plagues of Egypt?*
    The son of Rameses II
67. *What was his name?*
    Menephthah.
68. *When did the decline of Egypt begin?*
    In the 7th century B. C., when it was conquered by the Assyrians.
69. *Who revived the Egyptian power?*
    Psammeticus and his successor Necho, who completely subdued all the enemies.
70. *What great event occurred during Necho's reign?*
    The circumnavigation of Africa.
71. *What other country besides Egypt did Necho rule?*
    All the country between the Mediterranean Sea and the River Euphrates.
72. *How did Necho lose his possessions in Asia?*
    By his defeat in the battle of Carchemish.
73. *Who commanded the victorious army in this battle?*
    Nebuchadnezzar.
74. *When did Egypt pass into the control of the Persians?*
    In the 6th century, when they were conquered by Cambyses, and became a part of the Persian Empire.

75. *When did Egypt throw off the Persian yoke?*
   Under Alexander the Great, 334 B. C.
76. *What did Alexander do in Egypt?*
   Built a new city, Alexandria, at the mouth of the Nile.
77. *Who was the father of Alexander?*
   King Philip of Macedon.
78. *What happened to Egypt after the death of Alexander?*
   It passed into the rule of the Ptolemies from 323 B. C. to 30 B. C.
79. *Name some improvements in Egypt during the reign of Ptolemy I.*
   The erection of magnificent buildings, among them a white marble lighthouse, called the Pharos, one of the seven wonders of the world, and the founding of the greatest library of the ancient world at Alexandria.
80. *What special volume did the Alexandrian library contain?*
   A translation of the Hebrew Scriptures into Greek.
81. *What was this translation called?*
   The Septuagint.
82. *Why so named?*
   Because there were seventy persons who translated it from the Hebrew.
83. *How many Ptolemies were there?*
   Thirteen in all.
84. *Who was the last Ptolemy?*
   Cleopatra, a brilliant princess.
85. *What happened during her reign?*
   Egypt was conquered by Rome.
86. *How did Cleopatra come to her death?*
   She killed herself rather than be seen in the triumphal procession of her Roman conqueror, Octavius.
87. *When did Egypt come into the control of the Romans?*
   In the year 30 B. C.

88. *How long did Rome control Egypt?*
    Until the Fall of the Roman Empire.

89. *Who has controlled Egypt since the Fall of the Roman Empire?*
    The Turks, principally.

90. *What is the title of the Ruler of Egypt?*
    Khedive.

91. *What were the rulers called from 1250 to 1517?*
    The Mameluke Sultans.

92. *Who conquered the Turks at the end of the 18th century?*
    The French under Bonaparte.

93. *What was Bonaparte's charge to his soldiers at the Battle of the Pyramids?*
    "Soldiers! from yonder pyramids forty centuries look down upon you."

94. *How long did Egypt remain under French rule?*
    The French were expelled by the English in 1802, and the province was restored to Turkey.

95. *Mention two powerful rulers of Egypt after this period.*
    Mehemet Ali and his grandson Ismail Pasha, the first of the Khedives.

96. *What great undertaking was attempted by Ismail Pasha?*
    The conquest of Central Africa called the Soudan, and the suppression of the slave trade.

97. *What Englishman was appointed governor of the Soudan in the service of the Khedive?*
    General Gordon, in 1874.

98. *What great revolt against Egyptian power took place in Soudan?*
    The revolt of the Mahdi.

99. *What is the meaning of Mahdi?*
    According to Mohammedan belief, a spiritual ruler who is to appear on earth during the last days.

100. *Who had himself proclaimed as Mahdi?*
    Mohammed Ahmed, a man of low birth.
101. *What did he do?*
    He gathered an insurgent band of Mohammedans around him, and the tide of insurrection was a source of serious peril to Egypt.
102. *What was the fate of Gordon?*
    He was besieged by the Mahdi at Khartoum, and killed in the storming of the city, 1885.
103. *Name some great curiosities in Egypt.*
    Pyramids, Sphinxes, Obelisks, etc.
104. *Where are the Pyramids?*
    In the western valley of the Nile, from near Cairo to about 100 miles up the river.
105. *How many Pyramids were there at first?*
    Over 100, and 65 yet remain.
106. *What was the purpose of the Pyramids?*
    Monuments over the remains of noted rulers.
107. *What is the shape of the Pyramids?*
    Four-sided, directed toward the Cardinal Points.
108. *Give dimensions of the largest Pyramid.*
    Each side of base 746 feet, height 450 feet.
109. *Of what material are the Pyramids built?*
    Stone, or a mass of rubble with an external casing of stone.
110. *Do they still maintain their original size?*
    They do not; they are often partially destroyed for their building material.
111. *What is a Sphinx?*
    A fabulous monster of mythology.
112. *What were the Sphinxes of Egypt?*
    Large statues representing the head of a man and the body of a lion.

113. *What is an Obelisk?*
    A large shaft of stone, usually square, and covered with hieroglyphics.
114. *Where are they most numerous?*
    In Egypt.
115. *What has been done with some of them?*
    Presented to different nations for monuments or statues.
116. *Has the United States received any?*
    There was one presented to the City of New York by the Khedive of Egypt.
117. *How has the history of ancient Egypt been preserved?*
    By the hieroglyphics on the walls of the palaces, temples, monuments and tombs.
118. *What are Hieroglyphics?*
    A series of pictures and characters symbolizing ideas, letters, syllables and words.
119. *How did their meaning become known to the scholars of to-day?*
    Through the discovery of the Rosetta Stone, one of the greatest discoveries of modern times.
120. *What is the Rosetta Stone?*
    An Egyptian tablet discovered at Rosetta and containing an inscription written in both hieroglyphics and Greek. By comparing the two, Champollion, a celebrated French scientist, found the meaning of a few characters and from that beginning the whole of the ancient Egyptian writing has been deciphered.
121. *On what was Egyptian literature written?*
    On scrolls of papyrus or paper reed, which flourished luxuriantly in ancient times on the banks of the Nile.
122. *What is the most celebrated Egyptian book?*
    The Book of the Dead, a ritual for the use of the soul in its journey after death. A copy was enclosed in every mummy case.

123. *How did the Egyptians care for their dead?*
 They embalmed them and placed various articles in the tombs with them; especially images of the deceased persons and utensils connected with their profession or trade.
124. *What did the religion of ancient Egypt teach?*
 A judgment after death, immortality and transmigration of the soul; and it had many gods growing out of One.
125. *What was its form?*
 A ceremonial worship of animals as emblems of Deity.

CHINA.

1. *Where is the Chinese Empire and what does it embrace?*
 In the central part of Asia, and it embraces China proper or the Middle Kingdom and its chief dependencies of Mongolia, Manchuria, Thibet, Sungaria and East Turkestan.
2. *What is the area of the Empire?*
 One-fourth of Asia, or a little more than one-thirteenth of the land area of the globe.
3. *What is the relation of the population of the Chinese Empire to its commerce?*
 Although the Empire is as large as the United States and Mexico and has nearly six times their population, its commerce does not equal that of Switzerland.
4. *What is meant by China Proper?*
 The fertile valleys drained by the Ho-ang-ho and Yang-ste-kiang Rivers.

5. *What other name has the Ho-ang-ho River?*
   Yellow River, on account of its color.
6. *What is there peculiar about this river?*
   Frequent floods often cause a change in the channel, and sometimes divide it into two streams.
7. *On account of the destruction by its floods, what is it sometimes called?*
   "The Sorrow of China."
8. *What is the population of China?*
   Nearly 400,000,000.
9. *What follows from such an immense population?*
   The field of labor at home is so overcrowded that great numbers emigrate to every country that will receive them.
10. *What countries have refused to receive them?*
    The United States and the Australian provinces.
11. *What is said of the poverty of the people?*
    The masses of the population are poor with a poverty of which we have very little conception.
12. *Where is the Plateau of Thibet?*
    In the central part of China.
13. *What may be said of its height?*
    It is the highest land in the world inhabited by man.
14. *What is peculiar about the Inhabitants?*
    It is the only country in the world where Polyandry is legalized.
15. *What is meant by Polyandry?*
    A plurality of husbands.
16. *What is the origin of the Chinese?*
    Their records claim to read far back of all known chronology and are largely mythical.
17. *What part seems to be true?*
    The ancestors of the Chinese were wandering shepherds who gradually moved eastward from some point in Central Asia.

18. *What is supposed to be the date of the foundation of the Empire?*
   About 2800 B. C.
19. *Who was the great Social Teacher of the Chinese?*
   Fuh-hi, who established the law of marriage and introduced the written characters. He is said to have reigned 115 years and his tomb is shown at this day.
20. *What invention was made during his successor's rule?*
   The plow.
21. *Under whose reign was the Chinese territory greatly extended?*
   Under Tao, who began his reign about 2356 B. C.
22. *What improvements were made during Tao's reign?*
   Fairs were established, and flooded lands drained.
23. *What may be said of the successors of Tao?*
   They were cruel, vicious, and degenerate.
24. *What effect did their reign have on China?*
   The country degenerated, and civilization gave way to nomadic life.
25. *How long did this continue?*
   Till about 1100 B. C.
26. *What was the next Dynasty?*
   The Chow Dynasty.
27. *How long did the Chow Dynasty last?*
   From 1100 B. C. to 256 B. C.
28. *What did one of the early rulers of the Chow Dynasty do?*
   He divided the kingdom into a number of independent states that he might bestow principalities on his own relations.
29. *Who finally gained the ascendancy?*
   The kings of Tsin, and at last one of them reduced the other states to subjection and assumed the title of Hoang, Emperor.

30. *What gave the country its name?*
    The Tsin Dynasty, Tsina or China.
31. *How was the country disturbed in early times?*
    By incursions of Tartars.
32. *Who expelled them from China?*
    The first emperor, Che-Hwang-te, the national hero.
33. *What great work did Che-Hwang-te accomplish?*
    He began the Great Wall of China along the northern frontier as a protection against the hordes of barbarians.
34. *Give short description of the Wall.*
    Averages 25 feet high and 20 feet thick, with brick towers at regular intervals; is doubled at important passes, and is still in well-preserved condition. It extends over mountains and valleys twelve hundred miles and more. Earth enclosed in brickwork forms the mass of the wall, but for more than half its length it is little else than a heap of gravel and rubbish.
35. *What order was issued by Che-Hwang-te?*
    That all books and literature be burned.
36. *Why did he require this?*
    The people's admiration of the heroes of the earlier times was disastrous to the government and it seemed necessary to him that the past history of the Empire should be destroyed.
37. *How many Dynasties of Kings have ruled China?*
    Over twenty.
38. *Who were the constant terror of the Chinese?*
    The Mongolians or Tartars.
39. *When did they get a foothold in the Empire?*
    In 386 A. D., when they established an independent kingdom in the northern part of the Empire.
40. *From this time on what may be said of the Empire?*
    It was a constant struggle between the Tartars and the Chinese.

41. *What was the final result of these conflicts?*
    The conquest of the Empire by the Tartars, and the establishment of a Mongolian Dynasty.
42. *When was the first Mongolian Dynasty?*
    In the thirteenth century, when the great Asiatic conqueror Kublai Khan invaded the Empire.
43. *How long did it last?*
    One hundred years.
44. *What event took place during his reign?*
    The first European visited China.
45. *Who was the European who first went to China?*
    Marco Polo, in 1290 A. D. He remained there seventeen years and brought home a glowing description of the Eastern monarch's court.
46. *What occurred in the 17th century?*
    The Tartars again obtained the throne.
47. *What did they found?*
    The dynasty which still governs the empire, the Ta Tsing Dynasty.
48. *What was the opium war (1840)?*
    The trade in opium between China and Great Britain was not legalized and the Chinese Commissioner attempted to suppress it. This brought on unfriendly relations and war was declared between the two countries. The Chinese were thoroughly humbled by the result and sued for peace. A treaty was effected and by one of its provisions Hong Kong was ceded to the Queen.
49. *With whom did China carry on war between 1856 and 1860?*
    England and France.
50. *What was the cause of the war?*
    The impossibility of satisfactory relations with the Chinese government, because all foreigners were treated as inferiors, the Emperor and his officials claiming for China the sovereignty of the world.

51. *What was the result?*
 The allied powers made their own terms, and England established her right to have an envoy in Peking whether the Chinese liked it or not.
52. *How did the British punish the Chinese for perfidy?*
 They destroyed the Summer Palace. It covered an area of many miles and was filled with all the curiosities and treasures Chinese wealth and taste could bring together.
53. *What rebellion was inaugurated in 1850?*
 The Taiping Rebellion.
54. *What did the instigator pretend?*
 Calling himself the Heavenly Prince, he pretended that he had a mission to overturn the ruling dynasty and set up a purely native one, to be styled the Taiping or Great Peace Dynasty.
55. *How did the Taipings show their disloyalty to the government?*
 By discarding the queue, and they were on that account called long-haired rebels.
56. *When was the insurrection suppressed?*
 In 1864, with the aid of the Ever-victorious Army under Colonel Gordon, who from that time became known as "Chinese Gordon."
57. *Who is the present Emperor of China?*
 Kwang-Si, born in 1871.
58. *What is the sign of loyalty to the Government?*
 The wearing of the queue.
59. *Are the Chinese a wandering race?*
 They are not, but are home-loving, and when they emigrate it is with the expectation of returning to their "Flowery Land."
60. *Why has China influenced history so little?*
 Because the Chinese have kept themselves isolated from other nations.

CHINA.

61. *What is the cause of this?*
   Law and tradition.
62. *How is the life of the Chinese regulated?*
   The dress, the plan of the house, the mode of bowing, the minutest detail of life are regulated by three thousand ceremonial laws of immemorial usage.
63. *What is the chief occupation of the Chinese?*
   Agriculture.
64. *How is their respect for Agriculture shown?*
   Once a year, the Emperor exhibits himself in public holding a plow, with which he traces a furrow.
65. *What is said of their agricultural system?*
   It is rude but effective, and every inch of arable land is carefully cultivated.
66. *What do the Chinese call their country?*
   The "Flowery Land," or the "Flowery Kingdom."
67. *Name some articles that originated among the Chinese.*
   Tea, Silk, Paper, Printing, Magnetic Needle, and Gunpowder.
68. *How early was Astronomy cultivated by them?*
   As early as 2300 B. C. A Chinese chart of the stars represents the heavens as seen at that time.
69. *What is the comparative age of the Chinese language?*
   It is the oldest spoken language now existing upon the earth.
70. *Why is it called a monosyllabic language?*
   Because it has no alphabet, and each character represents in itself a complete idea.
71. *Why is it a difficult language to learn?*
   It is composed of an enormous list of characters, and each one must be learned by itself.
72. *What is said of the literature of the Chinese?*
   It is very extensive.

73. *What books are chiefly used in the schools?*
   The writings of Confucius. They are the model and type of all Chinese literary work.
74. *How is education regarded?*
   The public sentiment in favor of it is universal, and it is a reproach to any parents, however poor, if they neglect to send their sons to school.
75. *On what are appointments to the civil service based?*
   On examinations that include the preparation of essays and poems, and the writing of classical selections.
76. *What is the character of the government?*
   It is a patriarchal despotism, of which the family is the type. The emperor is the father of the nation, and his power is no more despotic than that with which the head of every family is clothed.
77. *What is the theory of parental authority in China?*
   The parent is the absolute master of his son, entitled to his service and obedience so long as the parent lives.
78. *What is the most essential duty?*
   Filial piety.
79. *How is the emperor assisted in administering the government?*
   He delegates his parental authority to officers of various ranks and degrees, and each of them becomes by this act the father of those under his jurisdiction.
80. *How must they administer justice?*
   So that no complaints are lodged against them at Peking.
81. *What is the important element in the conservation of this system?*
   The officers of state are chosen from among the people themselves, no class being entitled to special privileges from the emperor.

82. *What are some of the rewards given for ability in public service?*
    A peacock feather, to be worn in the official hat and possessed of no eye, or of one, two or three eyes, according to the magnitude of the favor shown; permission to enter the outer gate of the palace on horseback; a sable robe; and most prized of all, a short jacket of imperial yellow, the color sacred to His Majesty.
83. *Who was the great Philosopher of China?*
    Confucius.
84. *Give a short biography of Confucius.*
    Born June 19, 551 B. C.; lost his father when three years of age; was educated by his mother; set himself up as a teacher at the age of thirty; was a great teacher of religious truth, and holds a similar relation to China that Moses does to the western civilization. Died 479 B. C.—*American Cyclopedia.*
85. *How is he regarded by the people?*
    His memory is venerated and his word is law. He is the great arbitrator, authority and peacemaker of the empire.
86. *What worship is universal in China?*
    The worship of ancestors; it is as old as the race.
87. *What is the one original religion of China?*
    Confucianism.
88. *What other two religions supplement it?*
    Taoism and Buddhism.
89. *What is Confucianism?*
    The practical government of man through a code of morals, having reference solely to his present state.
90. *What is Taoism?*
    A religion of the supreme reason alone.

91. *Who taught it?*
    Laon-tsze, a celebrated philosopher who lived during the time of Confucius.
92. *When was Buddhism introduced into China?*
    During the 1st century. It spread rapidly and to day has more adherents than the other religions.
93. *Who performs the religious ceremonies?*
    The Emperor is the sole high priest and is the only one who, assisted by his ministers, can perform the great religious ceremonies, one of which is the sacrifice to Heaven every year at the time of the winter solstice.
94. *What was China called by Mediæval Europe?*
    Cathay.

JAPAN.

1. *Where is the Empire of Japan?*
   East of central Asia.
2. *What does it comprise?*
   Four large islands, and over three thousand small ones.
3. *What is the name of the largest island?*
   Niphon or Nipon.
4. *What is the meaning of the word Japan?*
   "Sunrise," or "the land of sunrise," and thus denotes the position the Empire occupies in the extreme East.
5. *Name the oldest books of Japanese History.*
   "Book of Traditions," published 712 A. D., and "Chronicles of Japan," published 720 A. D.
6. *What do these books record?*
   Besides giving account of events, they record the Japanese theory of creation.

7. *What is their Theory of Creation?*
   It is a rude specimen of evolution: that Heaven and Earth evolved from an egg, and that the Deity evolved from the Earth.
8. *From the best authority, what is thought to be the origin of the Japanese?*
   The weight of history is in favor of the idea that they migrated from north-eastern Asia, through Corea, to Japan.
9. *What is the legend of the pedigree of their sovereign?*
   There first existed seven generations of heavenly deities, who were followed by five generations of earthly deities, who in turn were succeeded by the mortal sovereigns, of whom the present Mikado or emperor is the 122nd.
10. *What is the earliest date accepted by the Japanese themselves?*
    One that corresponds to 660 B. C., when the first emperor, Jimmu, succeeded to the throne. It is styled the year 1, of the Japanese era.
11. *When did Buddhism enter Japan?*
    In the year 552 A. D.
12. *What effect did this have on Japan?*
    Chinese institutions were introduced, and a stream of skilled artisans, scholars, teachers, and missionaries poured into the country.
13. *What religious custom was adopted by the rulers?*
    That of abdicating the throne in order to spend old age in prayer.
14. *To what did this lead?*
    To the effacement of the Mikado's authority during the middle ages.
15. *What governmental changes occurred in 604 A. D.?*
    A Monarchical Government was established.
16. *What caused this change?*
    An acquaintance with the Chinese.

17. *How were the Officials divided?*
    Into civil and military grades; a regular system of ministers responsible to the sovereign, who, as Son of Heaven, was theoretically absolute.
18. *What war raged in the 10th century?*
    The war of the Red and White Flags.
19. *Why so called?*
    On account of the color of their banners.
20. *Was it a Civil or National War?*
    Civil, being between the ruling families.
21. *What title was conferred by the Mikado upon the conqueror?*
    Shogun, which signifies Greatest General, or General-in-Chief.
22. *What did the Shogun acquire in 1192?*
    The entire control of political affairs.
23. *What did the Mikado retain?*
    The religious supremacy and the symbols of royalty, and remained the theoretical head of the government.
24. *What grew up under this dual form of government?*
    A feudal-system, the military leaders or daimios securing land in fief, erecting castles and supporting a host of retainers.
25. *How long did this condition of affairs last?*
    Until 1868, when a revolution restored the Mikado to supreme power, destroyed the Shogun's rule and abolished the feudal titles and tenures.
26. *Who came to Japan during the 16th century?*
    The Portuguese.
27. *Who introduced Christianity?*
    Francis Xavier, the Apostle to the Indies, and in time, six hundred thousand converts were made.

28. *What did the Jesuit fathers accomplish?*
They founded churches, organized hospitals, and established colleges where the candidates for the church could be educated.
29. *What was the extent of their influence?*
At one time it seemed probable that Japan, as a nation, would embrace the Roman Catholic faith.
30. *What excited the alarm of the government at last?*
The intrigues of the missionaries.
31. *Who is regarded by the Japanese as their greatest man?*
Taiko-Sama.
32. *What edict did he issue?*
An edict expelling all foreign religious leaders.
33. *What is said of the persecution that followed?*
It has never been surpassed for cruelty and brutality on the part of the persecutors, or for courage and constancy on the part of those who suffered.
34. *What foreign people were still allowed to remain?*
The Dutch, who had come in 1600, were allowed a residence upon an island in the harbor of Nagasaki, and to exchange a single ship load of merchandise per year.
35. *How long did the government maintain its isolation?*
Until the country was opened to the five great western powers by the American treaty of March 31, 1854.
36. *What expedition secured it?*
The United States expedition, under Commodore Perry.
37. *What has the government of Japan become?*
A constitutional monarchy with a Cabinet, a Privy Council, a House of Peers, and a House of Representatives.
38. *What has been accomplished by the new order?*
Absolute religious freedom is secured, elementary education made compulsory, kindergarten methods are provided, and a flourishing government university is supported.

39. *What was the cause of the war between Japan and China in 1894-'95.*
A revolution in Corea drove the king into exile in Japan, and the latter nation landed a large number of troops on Corean soil. China resented this invasion, and upon the failure of the two nations to agree regarding their mutual relations toward Corea, war was declared, June, 1894.

40. *What was the result?*
Both countries sent large bodies of troops into Corea, and the Japanese were victorious. A treaty of peace was signed March 19, 1895, with terms favorable to Japan.

41. *What is the religious belief of the Japanese?*
The Shinto and the Buddhist. There are various Christian missions in Japan, principally in Tokio and Yokohama.

42. *What is the Shinto belief?*
A system of nature and hero worship. Its gods number fourteen thousand, and are propitiated by offerings of food and by music and dancing.

43. *What is peculiar about the Japanese written language?*
There are two distinct alphabets and kinds of writing in use; the system of Chinese hieroglyphic symbols which dates from the 3rd century, and a phonetic alphabet of forty-seven characters invented in the 9th century.

44. *What is said of the literature of Japan?*
It is abundant and various, and includes works on history and science, encyclopædias, poetry, prose, fiction, and translations of European works.

45. *What is the nature of Japanese art?*
It is essentially decorative, and in its application to a great degree purely industrial. One of its characteristic features is individuality of character in the treatment, by which the absence of all uniformity and monotony or sameness is secured.

46. *What is said of the governmental changes of Japan?*
A single generation has witnessed changes that required in Europe centuries to perfect.

BABYLONIA.

1. *Where was the Babylonian Empire?*
   In south-western Asia, along the Euphrates and Tigris Rivers.
2. *By what name is it known at present?*
   The Province of Bagdad.
3. *What other names have been given to the same territory?*
   "The Plains of Shinar" (Gen. x. 10); "The Plain of the Sea," etc.
4. *What is the source of the richness of the soil?*
   The overflow of the Euphrates and Tigris.
5. *What is said of their alluvial deposit?*
   It was marvellously fertile. In it wheat grew so rank that people mowed it twice to make it ear. The yield was from fifty to a hundred fold.
6. *What is the Euphrates sometimes called?*
   "The Nile of Babylon."
7. *What was another name for Babylonia?*
   Chaldea.
8. *What is known of the antiquity of Chaldea?*
   Recent archæological discoveries point to the remote date of 3,800 B. C., for a king Sargon I. who built palaces and temples, and founded libraries.
9. *What is known of the history of Chaldea?*
   The people were conquered by their northern neighbors, the Assyrians, in the 13th century, B. C., and they remained in servitude for several hundred years.

10. *What was the capital of Assyria?*
    Nineveh.
11. *What was the chief city of the Empire?*
    Babylon.
12. *When did the Chaldeans become masters of Babylon?*
    They captured Nineveh in 606 B. C., and Babylon, after the ruin of its rival, again became the capital of the East.
13. *Who were the Chaldeans?*
    They were the highest caste in Babylonia.
14. *What were their national powers?*
    They decided politics, commanded the armies, and held the chief offices.
15. *What may be said of the education of the Chaldeans?*
    They were highly educated. Astronomical calculations taken by them as far back as 2000 B. C. were found to be correct. They were also astrologers, they interpreted dreams and omens, gave instruction in the art of magic and conducted pompous religious ceremonies.
16. *When did they lose their power?*
    When Babylon was destroyed by Cyrus 538 B. C.
17. *What was the location of Babylon?*
    On the River Euphrates, 300 miles from its junction with the Tigris.
18. *What is the modern name?*
    The City Hillah, which was built out of its ruins, and near the ancient site of Babylon, in the year 1101.
19. *What was used for building material in the Empire?*
    Brick made of the native clay.
20. *What was the Median Wall?*
    A great wall, built of brick, on the northern boundary of the Empire from the Euphrates to the Tigris.
21. *What may be said of the Canals?*
    The country was an entire net-work of canals, used to convey the water to the already rich fields and gardens.

22. *What are these Canals called in Biblical literature?*
    The "Rivers of Babylon," where the captive Jews hung their harps on the willows along their banks, and wept over the desolation of Zion.
23. *What was the size of the city?*
    Fifteen miles square. It was larger than any modern city of the world.
24. *What was the most important building of Babylon?*
    The Palace of Nebuchadnezzar.
25. *When was it built?*
    Six hundred years B. C.
26. *What was the size of the Palace?*
    Six miles in circumference.
27. *What great structure was considered a wonder of the world?*
    The Hanging Gardens.
28. *Why were they built?*
    For the gratification of the Queen, who longed for mountain scenery.
29. *How were they built?*
    An artificial mountain was made, 400 feet high, and terraced on all sides. These terraces were sustained by piers, the whole being bound together by a wall 22 feet thick.
30. *What were planted on these terraces?*
    Large trees and flowers.
31. *How were the plants watered?*
    Water was drawn by machinery from the River Euphrates.
32. *Who was the Queen for whom all this was built?*
    Amytis, the Queen of Nebuchadnezzar.
33. *Did Nebuchadnezzar extend his territory?*
    He did; from Persia on the east to Egypt on the west.
34. *What captivity occurred in his reign?*
    The captivity of the Jews.

35. *Who was the last King of Babylon?*
   Belshazzar.
36. *How was Belshazzar's reign brought to a close?*
   By the invasion of Cyrus and the destruction of the city, 538 B. C.
37. *What country governed the Babylonian Empire subsequent to the year 538 B. C.?*
   It passed into the control of the Medo-Persian Empire.
38. *What was the writing of the Chaldeans?*
   Wedge-shaped characters.
39. *What are they called?*
   Cuneiform letters, from Cuneus a wedge.
40. *Upon what were they made?*
   Clay tablets, as there was no stone in Chaldea.
41. *How many characters have been deciphered?*
   Three hundred, and a large number still remain unknown.
42. *Describe a Babylonian book.*
   It consisted of several flat, square, clay tablets written on both sides and piled one upon another in order.
43. *What is said of the Chaldean account of the Creation and the Deluge?*
   They are like the narrative in Genesis, though written hundreds of years before Moses was born.
44. *How did the early Chaldeans bury their dead?*
   In large clay jars or in dish-covered tombs.
45. *What is told of some of the industries of Babylonia?*
   Their carpets were celebrated throughout the ancient world, and the elaborate designs of their embroideries served as models for the earliest Grecian urns.

PERSIA AND PALESTINE.

1. *Where is Persia?*
   In south-western Asia, south of the Caspian Sea.
2. *What is the native name of Persia?*
   Iran.
3. *Into how many States or Provinces is it divided?*
   Twenty-two large and ten small ones.
4. *What is the Capital and largest city?*
   Teheran.
5. *What is the Biblical name for Persia?*
   Elam.
6. *Who founded the Persian Empire, and when?*
   Cyrus the Great, in the sixth century B. C.
7. *What was its extent?*
   It reached from the Ægean Sea to India, beyond the Euphrates.
8. *What did it include?*
   Media, Assyria, Babylon, Asia Minor and Syria.
9. *By whom was he succeeded?*
   His son, Cambyses.
10. *What was the chief event of the reign of Cambyses?*
    The invasion and conquest of Egypt in a single battle.
11. *What stratagem did he use?*
    He placed before the army cats, dogs, and other animals sacred to the Egyptians.

12. *How did the Persians regard these two kings?*
    They called Cyrus, "Father," and Cambyses, "Despot."
13. *Who was called the second founder of the Persian Empire?*
    Darius I.
14. *What did he accomplish?*
    He perfected the organization of the empire, dividing it into twenty-three provinces, over which he placed governors, called by the Persians, satraps.
15. *Who was the son and successor of Darius?*
    Xerxes.
16. *What great invasion did Xerxes attempt?*
    To conquer Greece.
17. *Was he successful?*
    He was not. Terrified by the destruction of his fleet, he fled into Asia.
18. *What effect did this failure have on Xerxes?*
    He gave up to luxury, and was finally murdered by two of his servants in the year 465 B. C.
19. *What great change took place in the year 331 B. C.?*
    The empire became a Grecian province.
20. *Who produced this change?*
    Alexander the Great.
21. *What is the present government of Persia?*
    It is an Absolute Monarchy.
22. *What is the title of the ruler?*
    King, or Shah.
23. *What one thing limits the power of the Shah?*
    His inability to set aside any of the accepted doctrines of Mohammedanism.
24. *What were the characteristics of the Persians?*
    Originally they were a hardy race, of simple manners and great courage in war. In later days, they grew to be luxurious and effeminate.

PERSIA AND PALESTINE.

25. *What was the great end of Persian education?*
    To ride, to draw the bow and to speak the truth.
26. *What was notable in their architecture?*
    Broad, sculptured staircases, and tall, slender columns.
27. *What wonderful ruins are in Persia?*
    Persepolis, the magnificent capital of the ancient empire, consisting now of fragments of the palaces of Xerxes, Cyrus, and Darius and the royal tombs.
28. *What was the religion of the early Persians?*
    A simple worship of the Spirit of Good, and a belief in an Evil Spirit, to be hated and shunned.
29. *What did it become later?*
    The people became converts to the religion of Zoroaster and worshiped the element of fire under priests called Magi.
30. *What is said of the power of the national customs of ancient Persia?*
    The King was bound by them as closely as his subjects; his command, once given, could not be revoked even by himself, hence arose the phrase, "Unchangeable as the laws of the Medes and Persians."
31. *Where was ancient Palestine?*
    A part of Syria, lying between the desert on the east and the Mediterranean Sea.
32. *By what other names is it known?*
    Holy Land, and sometimes Judea.
33. *How many divisions in Palestine?*
    Four.
34. *What are they?*
    Galilee, Samaria, Judea, and the elevated district east of the Jordan.
35. *Which was the most important Province?*
    Judea.

36. *What was the Capital of Palestine?*
    Jerusalem.
37. *Who made it the Capital?*
    King David.
38. *Why was it called Palestine?*
    It is derived from the Hebrew word Philistia.
39. *What is the principal river?*
    The Jordan.
40. *Describe the River Jordan.*
    It rises in the Lebanon Mountains, and, after flowing 13 miles, enters Lake Tiberias, which is 620 feet above the level of the sea; then flowing south a distance of 100 miles, it enters the Dead Sea, which is 1,300 feet below the level of the Mediterranean.
41. *What was Palestine called in ancient times?*
    The Land of Canaan.
42. *What do we know of the early history of the Hebrews?*
    Abram, founder of the Hebrews, came from Chaldea about 2000 B. C.; they lived like the Arabs of to-day, in tents with their flocks and herds. Later generations were invited to settle in Egypt, where they were subsequently greatly oppressed, and finally rescued from bondage by Moses.
43. *Who accomplished the conquest of Palestine?*
    Joshua, the successor to Moses, destroyed thirty-one cities of Canaan in six years of hard fighting, and allotted the country to the twelve tribes of Israel.
44. *Name the three greatest kings of Israel.*
    Saul, David, and Solomon; each reigned forty years.
45. *Who was Saul?*
    The first king of Israel, chosen of God through the prophet Samuel.
46. *What was the character of David's reign?*
    He enlarged the boundaries of Palestine, fixed the capital at Jerusalem, organized an army, and enforced the worship of Jehovah as the national religion.

47. *Describe the reign of Solomon.*
    It was the most splendid period of Jewish history. He built the great temple in Jerusalem, erected magnificent palaces, and sent expeditions to India and Arabia.
48. *What occurred after Solomon's death?*
    The empire was rent into the petty kingdoms, Israel and Judah, the former containing ten tribes, the latter two.
49. *What was the fate of the kingdom of Israel?*
    It was idolatrous, and after much turmoil and many vicissitudes, the people vanished from history. They are known as the Lost Tribes.
50. *What happened to the kingdom of Judah?*
    It retained the national religion, and existed for nearly four hundred years. Then Nebuchadnezzar destroyed Jerusalem and sent the king and many of the inhabitants in chains to Babylon.
51. *What was the Restoration?*
    After a captivity of seventy years, the Jews were allowed by Cyrus to return to Judea and rebuild their temple.
52. *When was Jerusalem taken by Rome?*
    In 70 A. D., by Titus, after a siege of untold horror.
53. *What was done with the Jews?*
    They were scattered as slaves or exiles.
54. *Who has ruled Palestine most of the time since then?*
    The Saracens and Turks, both Mohammedans.
55. *What were the Crusades, and when did they occur?*
    They were pilgrimages made to Palestine during the Middle Ages by the people of Europe for the purpose of rescuing Jerusalem from Mohammedan power.
56. *Were they successful?*
    They were not.
57. *Who rules Palestine at present?*
    It is subject to the Turks.

58. *How has the Jewish nation influenced the world?*
   Its sacred books constitute the Bible, and its religion has molded the faith of the most civilized nations.
59. *What great interest has the Hebrew commonwealth for us?*
   It was the first republic of which we have definite knowledge.
60. *What was the character of the Mosaic laws?*
   They were mild and far beyond the spirit of the age.
61. *How was learning regarded by the Hebrews?*
   It was held in high esteem, and everyone received what we should call a common school education; also, every boy was compelled to learn a trade.

GREECE.

1. *Where is Greece?*
   The most eastern of three peninsulas which extend southward from Europe.
2. *How was ancient Greece divided?*
   Into three parts; the first, in the north, was composed of Thessaly and Epirus; the second, in the middle, called Hellas, which was the most important part; and the third, the peninsula forming the southern part called Peloponnesus.
3. *What can be said of the geographical features of Greece?*
   They had much to do with fixing the character of its inhabitants, the great variety of soil and climate tending to produce a versatile people.
4. *Describe the coast of Greece.*
   It is deeply indented with numerous bays having bold

promontories reaching far out to sea and forming excellent harbors.

5. *How did that affect the Greeks?*
It offered them every inducement to a sea-faring life.
6. *Describe the interior of Greece.*
The land is cut up by almost impassable mountain ranges.
7. *What was the effect upon the people?*
Each little valley, being isolated, developed its own peculiar life.
8. *Name four important Mountains in Greece.*
Olympus, 10,000 feet high; Parnassus, 8,000 feet high; Pentelieus, 4,000 feet high; and Hymettus, 3,400 feet high.
9. *What is the origin of the Greeks?*
They belong to the Aryan family, and are in close relation to the people of Central Asia.
10. *Who were the primitive inhabitants of Greece?*
The Pelasgians, a simple agricultural people.
11. *Who conquered the country?*
The Hellenes, a war-like race who gave the land its name, Hellas.
12. *What were the principal cities of Greece?*
Athens, Sparta, Corinth, and Thebes.
13. *When were these cities founded?*
About 1500 B. C.
14. *What was the earliest period of Grecian history called?*
The Heroic Age.
15. *Are the events of the Heroic Age authentic?*
They are not, but are clouded in mystery.
16 *When did Grecian Mythology originate?*
During the Heroic Age.
17. *Name two great Traditions of this Age.*
The Expedition of the Argos and the Trojan War.

18. *Name some noted persons belonging to the Heroic Age.*
    Hercules, Theseus, and Achilles.
19. *What is the first clearly defined event of Grecian history?*
    The Dorian Migration.
20. *What was it?*
    The Dorians, a hardy race from the north, invaded the Peloponnesus and made an entire conquest about the 11th century B. C.
21. *What is this movement called in history?*
    The Return of the Heracleidæ (Her-a-cli′de), as it was conducted by the descendants of Hercules who had been banished for more than a century.
22. *What was the other leading race in Greece?*
    The Ionians.
23. *What were the two great centers of Hellenic life?*
    Sparta, the capital of the Dorians, and Athens, the capital of the Ionians.
24. *What change was there in the names of these races?*
    Each was called after its capital, and are known as the Spartans and Athenians.
25. *What were the chief characteristics of the Spartans?*
    They were rough and plain in their habits, pitiless, fearless warriors in battle, and were enemies of trade and the fine arts.
26. *What were the characteristics of the Athenians?*
    They were refined in their tastes, democratic, commercial, and lovers of music, painting, and sculpture.
27. *Who is said to have introduced the Alphabet into Greece?*
    Cadmus, who brought it from Phoenicia.
28. *Why is the Second Age called Homeric?*
    Because Homer immortalized this Period by his poetry.
29. *When did Homer live?*
    Sometime between 1000 B. C., and 870 B. C.

30. *What are Homer's greatest poems?*
 The Iliad and the Odyssey.
31. *What criticism has been offered on the two poems of Homer?*
 That they were not written by one man, but were fragments of old poems collected by different persons.
32. *How have they been honored?*
 The cities of Greece owned state copies of his works which not even the treasures of kings could buy; and his poems were then, as now, the standard classics in a literary education.
33. *What great law-giver lived in this Period?*
 Lycurgus.
34. *What is said of Lycurgus?*
 He declined the Spartan Crown, and made the people swear to abide by his laws until his return; then he left the country, and died in another land.
35. *How were the people taught by Lycurgus?*
 To speak in short sentences; hence the Laconic style of language.
36. *What was the name of Sparta during his rule?*
 Laconia; hence the word laconic.
37. *Did the Greeks have any central government?*
 They did not, but necessity caused them to form treaties.
38. *What united all Greece in a sacred bond?*
 The Four Great National Games.
39. *How long did these Games last at a time?*
 For many days; similar to a County or State Fair.
40. *What were they?*
 Olympic, Pythian, Nemean, and Isthmian.
41. *Which was the greatest?*
 The Olympic.
42. *Describe the Olympic Games.*
 Held every four years at Olympia; races of all kinds were

engaged in, the ballads of Homer were recited, and the victor was crowned with a crown of olive, or laurel.

43. *Who contended in these Games?*
Greeks from all over the world, but no other nations.

44. *What effect did these sports have on military operations?*
All military operations ceased during their continuance.

45. *Who founded the Olympic Games?*
Tradition says, Hercules.

46. *What is meant by the "Olympiad?"*
As this festival occurred so regularly, it was used as a measure of time, the year 776 B. C. to 772 B. C. being the First Olympiad.

47. *What two States were the greatest contenders in these Games?*
Athens and Sparta.

48. *What was the next Festival of importance?*
The Pythian, in honor of the God Apollo.

49. *What was a special feature of the Pythian Festival?*
The contests of poetry, music, and oratory.

50. *When was it held?*
The third year of every Olympiad.

51. *Whose honor was celebrated by the Nemean Games?*
The Greek God Zeus.

52. *How often were they held?*
Every two years, near Cleonæ.

53. *Where were the Isthmian Games held?*
On the Isthmus of Corinth, near the Temple of Poseidon, the Sea God.

54. *What may be said of the Spartans at this time?*
They became masters of most of their near neighbors, and got control of the Peninsula.

55. *What may be said of Athens, the rival of Sparta?*
   Athens also increased in power and influence.
56. *Who gave a code of laws to Athens?*
   Draco.
57. *What is said of Draco's laws?*
   That they were written in blood.
58. *Why were they thus spoken of?*
   Because of their severity, the smallest offense being punishable by death.
59. *What did Draco say in defense of his laws?*
   "The smallest crime deserves death, and I can find no heavier penalty for the greatest."
60. *Who canceled Draco's severe laws?*
   Solon, who ruled at Athens from 594 to 560 B. C.
61. *When was the "Age of Tyranny," and why so called?*
   From 650 to 500 B. C ; because many of the cities were governed by despots.
62. *Who founded a Public Library at Athens?*
   Pisistratus, who ruled from 560 to 527 B. C.
63. *What institution was devised at this time to prevent future tyranny?*
   Ostracism.
64. *What was ostracism?*
   Any citizen could be banished without trial by a vote of the people, each citizen writing the name of the person whom he wished to banish on a shell (called ostracon), six thousand votes being required against the person to determine his condemnation.
65. *What was the original meaning of the word tyrant?*
   It was at first applied, by the Greeks, to a person who became king in a city where the law did not authorize one. Afterward the tyrant became cruel and the word took on the meaning we now give it.

66. *Who established a Democracy at Athens?*
   Cleisthenes.
67. *Where had Greece any Colonies?*
   In Asia Minor, Italy, and in Africa.
68. *When did Athens become a Republic?*
   In the year 510 B. C.
69. *What effect did this have on the Colonies?*
   The Asiatic Colonies revolted against Persia, who had lately subdued them.
70. *What did the Athenians do for the Colonies and what was the result?*
   They sent assistance which precipitated the Persian wars.
71. *Why called the Persian Wars?*
   Because for eleven years the Persians were trying to subdue Greece.
72. *Who was Ruler of Persia at this time?*
   Darius.
73. *Whom did Darius send with the army on the first invasion?*
   His son-in-law, Mardonius.
74. *What was the result of this invasion?*
   It was an entire failure; the fleet being wrecked off Mt. Athos and a large part of the army drowned.
75. *When was the second invasion?*
   In the year 490 B. C.
76. *Where did the two armies meet?*
   On the Plains of Marathon.
77. *What was the number of persons in each army?*
   Persians, over 100,000; Athenians, 10,000; an extraordinary disparity.
78. *What was the result of the battle?*
   The Persians were defeated and driven to their vessels, and they then sailed away.
79. *How is this conflict regarded?*
   As one of the world's greatest battles.

GREECE.   45

80. *Why?*
    If the Persians had succeeded, the character of European civilization would have been entirely changed, becoming Asiatic.
81. *How many Generals were in the Grecian Army at the Battle of Marathon?*
    Ten, each of whom had command for one day.
82. *Name three of the most noted Generals.*
    Aristides, Miltiades, and Themistocles.
83. *Who was considered the greatest?*
    Miltiades.
84. *What did each of the other Generals do?*
    They each resigned in favor of Miltiades.
85. *What is Miltiades called?*
    The "Hero of Marathon."
86. *What became of Miltiades?*
    He died in prison, of wounds received in a treasonable attack on the Island of Paros.
87. *How long was it until the next Invasion?*
    Ten years (480 B. C.).
88. *Who led the Invasion?*
    Xerxes, the son of Darius.
89. *How many men had Xerxes?*
    Over one million.
90. *Where did the armies meet?*
    At the Pass of Thermopylæ.
91. *Who met Xerxes at Thermopylæ?*
    Leonidas, with three hundred Spartan soldiers.
92. *What was the result of the battle?*
    Leonidas and all but two of his three hundred were slain.
93. *How large was Leonidas' entire army?*
    Six thousand persons.

94. *Where were they at the Battle of Thermopylæ?*
   He had dismissed all but the three hundred Spartans, and four hundred Thespians, who were in reserve.
95. *What caused his great defeat?*
   The treachery of a Greek, who admitted the Persians to a Pass.
96. *What did Xerxes do next?*
   He pressed on into Greece, and burnt Athens.
97. *Where was the next battle?*
   A naval one, off the Isle of Salamis.
98. *What was the result of this battle?*
   A great victory for the Grecians.
99. *How long did the battle last?*
   From morning till night.
100. *After this engagement, what did Xerxes do?*
   He withdrew, and returned to Persia in dismay.
101. *Did he take all his army?*
   He left Mardonius, with 300,000 men, in Thessaly.
102. *What became of Mardonius?*
   He was defeated and slain the next year at the Battle of Platea and Mycale.
103. *Who were the Grecian Generals in the battle of Platea?*
   Aristides and Pausanias.
104. *What effect did these Wars have on Persia?*
   No Persian army was ever again seen in Greece.
105. *What was Aristides called by his countrymen?*
   The Just, on account of his incorruptible character. Tradition says he was so honest he did not have enough to meet his funeral expenses.
106. *Who was the greatest Statesman of Athens?*
   Pericles.
107. *What is the period in which he lived sometimes called?*
   The "Age of Pericles."

108. *How long did he direct affairs at Athens?*
 For forty years (469–429 B. C.).
109. *What is said of his Administration?*
 It was the most splendid the Athenians ever had. Art and literature flourished, and the city was embellished with the most magnificent edifices.
110. *What military event took place in 431 B. C.?*
 The long-continued jealousy between Sparta and Athens broke out in war.
111. *What was this War called?*
 The Peloponnesian War.
112. *Who was the Spartan General in this War?*
 Lysander.
113. *What was the result of this War?*
 After twenty seven years of alternate victories and defeat, Athens fell.
114. *What may be said of Sparta?*
 It became the leading city of Greece.
115. *How did Sparta govern Athens?*
 By thirty men, sometimes called the thirty tyrants, on account of their cruelty.
116. *What did Athens do under the thirty tyrants?*
 Began to regain her political principles, and after the Athenians had been ruled eight months, they overthrew the tyrants and re-established a democratic government.
117. *What great man lived in Athens at this time?*
 Socrates.
118. *When was he born?*
 In 468 B. C.
119. *What crime was Athens guilty of in the year 399 B. C.?*
 The putting to death of Socrates.

120. *Why was he put to death?*
 On the false charge of introducing a new worship to corrupt the youth.

121. *On what condition was he offered his life?*
 That he would cease to teach.

122. *What great truth did he teach?*
 The immortality of the soul, the beauty and necessity of virtue, and the moral responsibility of man.

123. *How was he put to death?*
 He was sentenced to drink a cup of poison hemlock, which he took in his prison chamber, surrounded by his friends, with whom he cheerfully conversed till the last.

124. *Who were his most eminent disciples?*
 Plato and Xenophon, from whom we derive our knowledge of his doctrines, since he himself committed nothing to writing.

125. *What did Plato found?*
 The Academic School of Philosophy, so-called because he delivered his lectures in the Academic Gardens.

126. *By what is he best known?*
 By his arguments in regard to the immortality of the soul. He taught that death is to be desired rather than feared.

127. *What other great Schools of Philosophy were founded in the fourth century B. C.?*
 The Peripatetics, the Epicureans, and the Stoics.

128. *Who founded the Peripatetic School?*
 Aristotle, who was a student of Plato.

129. *Why so called?*
 Aristotle delivered his lectures while walking up and down the shady porches of the Lyceum, surrounded by his pupils (hence called Peripatetics, *walkers*).

GREECE.

130. *What has been the influence of Aristotle's teaching?*
He, more than any other philosopher, originated ideas whose influence is still felt. The "Father of Logic," the principles he laid down in his study have never been superseded.
131. *Who were the Epicureans?*
The followers of Epicurus.
132. *What did Epicurus teach?*
That the chief end of life is enjoyment. He was strictly moral and taught that virtue is the road to happiness, but his followers so perverted this that Epicurean became a synonym for loose and luxurious living.
133. *Who were the Stoics?*
They were the followers of Zeno.
134. *From what was their name derived?*
The painted portico (stoa) under which he taught.
135. *What was their belief?*
Pain and pleasure were equally despised by them, and indifference to all external conditions was considered the highest virtue.
136. *What is the name of the Historic Period from 371 to 361 B. C.?*
The Theban.
137. *Why called the Theban Period?*
Because of the war between the Spartans and Thebans.
138. *Who was the leading General of Thebes?*
Epaminondas.
139. *What famous battle was fought?*
The battle of Leuctra.
140. *What was the result of this battle?*
The defeat of the Spartans for the first time in their history.
141. *When was this battle fought?*
In the year 371 B. C.

142. *What did Sparta do after the battle?*
   Sent embassadors to Athens to solicit aid.

143. *How long did Thebes rule Greece?*
   Until the death of Epaminondas, in the battle of Mantinea.

144. *When was the Battle of Mantinea fought?*
   In the year 362 B. C.

145. *What was the result of this battle?*
   With the death of the great leader the Theban cause died.

146. *What effect did these Civil and National Wars have on Greece?*
   The States were so exhausted that they were not able to withstand a very formidable invasion.

147. *Who were the next to invade Greece?*
   The Macedonians.

148. *What is this period called?*
   The Macedonian (362–146 B. C.).

149. *Who were the Macedonians?*
   Barbarians, who lived just north of Greece.

150. *What is meant by Barbarians?*
   The Greeks called all people who did not use their language Barbarians, or Babblers.

151. *What did the Macedonians say as to their own origin?*
   They claimed to be descendants of Hercules.

152. *What privileges did this give them?*
   They were admitted to the Olympic Games.

153. *Who was King of Macedon at this time?*
   Philip II., who had been a hostage at Thebes, and had learned the arts of war.

154. *Was King Philip well educated?*
   He was, and could speak the Greek language with great fluency.

GREECE.

155. *What did Philip proceed to do?*
 To make war against the Athenians.

156. *What was the result?*
 He defeated the Grecians in the great battle of Cheronea, August 7, 338 B. C.

157. *What did the Athenian Congress do?*
 They acknowledged the supremacy of Philip, and appointed him to command the Grecian Army in their proposed war against Persia.

158. *What became of Philip?*
 He was assassinated at a feast, at the age of forty-seven years.

159. *Who succeeded Philip?*
 His son, Alexander the Great.

160. *How old was Alexander at this time?*
 Twenty years.

161. *What did the Grecian Congress do?*
 Conferred on Alexander the same power they had on his father.

162. *What did Alexander then do?*
 With 35,000 Greeks he began his march to conquer the world.

163. *Was he successful?*
 He was, and became the Oriental Monarch.

164. *What did he do?*
 He conquered all Persia, and finally Tyre, and built the city of Alexandria, near the mouth of the Nile.

165. *Where and when did he die?*
 At Babylon, 323 B. C., age thirty-three years.

166. *After his death, what did Greece do?*
 It formed a Confederacy of States.

167. *Were they successful?*
 They were not, but were still under the control of Macedon.
168. *What great event happened to Greece in the year 168 B. C.?*
 It became a Roman Province.
169. *What was Greece called by the Romans?*
 The Province of Achaia.
170. *What great Orator lived at this time?*
 Demosthenes; born 385, died 322 B. C.
171. *Where did Demosthenes live?*
 In Athens.
172. *Was he naturally a fine speaker?*
 Was not; had a weak constitution and defective utterance.
173. *Was he wealthy?*
 Was left an orphan at the age of seven years, with some property, which was squandered by relatives.
174. *How did he become an Orator?*
 By striving to regain his property, and pleading for his rights before the Athenian courts.
175. *Was he successful?*
 At the age of twenty-one he regained a part of his property.
176. *What are his most noted Orations?*
 His Philippics.
177. *What were the Philippics?*
 Orations against the invasion of Philip.
178. *What did the Macedonians do with Demosthenes?*
 They threw him into prison, but he escaped by the aid of friends, and remained in exile until the death of Alexander.
179. *Did he ever return?*
 He did, but was again sought by the Macedonian King, Antipater.

180. *Where did he take refuge?*
    In the temple.
181. *Was he captured?*
    He carried with him poison, to prevent his capture, and before the officers of Antipater could capture him, he took from his own hand the fatal dose.
182. *What is the period from 146 B. C. to 395 A. D. called?*
    The Roman.
183. *What did the Romans do when they captured Greece?*
    They sacked and burnt the city of Corinth, which had been the capital of the Achaian League, and later Cæsar rebuilt it.
184. *What may be said of Athens?*
    It continued to be the seat of culture and education, and Roman scholars flocked there for its advantages.
185. *How were the Grecians now governed?*
    Entirely by Rome, for 541 years.
186. *When did Paul visit Greece?*
    About the year 50 A. D.
187. *Where did he dwell?*
    At Corinth, and followed his occupation of tent-making for two years.
188. *When was the Roman Capital removed and where?*
    In the year 330 A. D., to Byzantium, a Greek City, afterward known as Constantinople, Constantine's city.
189. *When and how was the Roman Empire divided?*
    In 395 A. D., into an Eastern and Western Empire.
190. *To which one did Greece belong?*
    On account of location, to the Eastern.
191. *What period now begins?*
    The Byzantine (395 to 1453 A. D.).

192. *What was the condition of Greece for the next one thousand years?*
Nothing of importance; a few invasions by Normans and Turks.

193. *What finally happened?*
In 1453, Mahomed II. took Byzantium, and conquered all Greece.

194. *What did Greece then become?*
A part of the Turkish Empire.

195. *What may be said of Greece under the Turks?*
The people were greatly oppressed and the country but little improved.

196. *When was the Greek Church established?*
During the Byzantine Period.

197. *Has there been any uprising against the Turks?*
One, in 1821, in which Lord Byron, the poet, took sides with the Greeks; but one-half the population is said to have perished and large tracts of land were reduced to a desert.

198. *What was the result?*
The Independence of Greece was proclaimed in 1822.

199. *What countries formed a league to assist Greece?*
England, Russia and France.

200. *Who is the present King?*
Prince George.

201. *When did he become King?*
In the year 1863.

202. *What was the religion of the ancient Greeks?*
A mythology which invested every stream, grove, and mountain with gods and goddesses, nymphs, and naiads.

203. *How were their deities worshiped?*
With songs and dances, dramas and festivals, spirited contests and gorgeous processions.

204. *Name three great Greek tragic poets?*
 Æschylus, Sophocles and Euripides.
205. *Name three historians.*
 Herodotus (called the Father of History), Thucydides and Xenophon.
206. *Name two great sculptors.*
 Phidias and Praxiteles.
207. *What are the three styles of Grecian architecture?*
 Doric, Ionic and Corinthian; distinguished by the shape of their columns.
208. *What celebrated ruin is at Athens?*
 The Parthenon, originally a temple sacred to Pallas Athene, the patron goddess of Athens.
209. *What is said of its sculptures?*
 The magnificent sculptures that adorned it were designed by Phidias. Some of them are now in the British Museum and are the finest in existence.

ROME.

1. *Where is Italy?*
 It is the central one of three great peninsulas that extend from the south of Europe into the Mediterranean Sea.
2. *What is the size of the Peninsula?*
 Length, 700 miles; width on the north, 350 miles, and in the south, 100 miles.—*Smith.*
3. *What sea bounds Italy on the east?*
 The Adriatic, called by the Romans "Mare Superum."
4. *What was Northern Italy called by the Romans?*
 Gallia Cisalpina.

5. *Why so called?*
   It meant the country inhabited by Gauls, on this side of the Alps.
6. *Into how many Classes are the early inhabitants divided?*
   Into three great classes: Italians, Iapygians, and Etruscans.
7. *What did the Italians inhabit?*
   The central part of Italy.
8. *Into what two branches were the Italians divided?*
   Latins and Umbro-Sabellians.
9. *What seems to have been the origin of the Italians?*
   It is evident that they are related to the Greeks, and at some remote period immigrated from the East.
10. *Where did the Iapygians dwell?*
    In the extreme south-eastern part of Italy.
11. *Who are they supposed to be?*
    The original inhabitants of Italy, who were driven to the South by the newcomers from the East.—*Smith.*
12. *Where did the Etruscans dwell?*
    In the northern part of Italy, between the Arno and the Tiber, a league of twelve cities. These people were great builders and skilled in the arts.
13. *Besides these three Races, who else settled in Italy in ancient times?*
    Greek colonists, and Gauls from the North.
14. *What general name finally included all the inhabitants of Italy?*
    Romans.
15. *When does trustworthy history of Rome begin?*
    About the year 281 B. C.
16. *Why no earlier than this?*
    About this time the Gauls sacked the city and destroyed the records, and it was five hundred years after the

founding of the city before the first rude attempt was made to write a continuous narrative of its origin.

17. *When was Rome founded, and where?*
    753 B. C., on the river Tiber, fifteen miles from its mouth.
18. *What did the Romans accept as the early history of Rome?*
    A series of legends.
19. *What is the legend of the birth of the founder of Rome?*
    Romulus and his twin brother Remus, children of the vestal virgin Rhea Silvia and the god Mars, were thrown into the Tiber. They were cast ashore at the foot of Mt. Palatine, nursed by a wolf, and finally rescued by a shepherd and brought up by him.
20. *What is the legend of the founding of Rome?*
    When the brothers were grown they determined to build a city near the spot where they had been so wonderfully preserved. Romulus desired to build on the Palatine Hill and Remus on the Aventine. The dispute was decided in favor of Romulus by the aid of the shepherds and he called the new city Rome after his own name and became its first king.
21. *What became of Remus?*
    He was slain by Romulus for jumping over the mud wall of the city in scorn. Romulus exclaimed as he slew him: "So perish every one who may try to leap over these ramparts."
22. *How did Romulus obtain inhabitants for the city?*
    By making Rome an asylum for murderers, slaves and thieves.
23. *How were women obtained for the city?*
    By kidnapping the Latin and Sabine virgins.
24. *What is the real history of the founding of Rome as received by the best critics?*
    It was founded by Latins as an outpost against the Etruscans, whom they greatly feared.

25. *What was its probable size at an early date?*
    It contained about one thousand miserable thatched huts surrounded by a wall.
26. *What were the inhabitants?*
    Most of them were shepherds or farmers who tilled the land upon the plain near by but lived for protection within the fortifications on the Palatine Hill.
27. *What was the early government?*
    It was aristocratic. It had a king, a senate and an assembly. Each family was represented in the senate by its head.
28. *What was the influence of the Senate?*
    It was from the beginning the soul of the city and shaped the public life of Rome throughout its entire history.
29. *What was the Sabine invasion and league?*
    The Sabines, a neighboring tribe, captured the Capitoline and Quirinal Hills. After frequent conflicts they came into alliance and formed one city.
30. *What are the people of the two tribes called?*
    Romans and Quirites.
31. *What were their rights?*
    Both had seats in the Senate and the king was taken alternately from each.
32. *Who was the first Sabine King?*
    Numa Pompilius, the successor of Romulus.
33. *What is said of his reign?*
    It was prosperous. He built the Temple of Janus and established religious institutions.
34. *Who succeeded Pompilius?*
    Tullus Hostilius, 673 to 641 B. C.
35. *What may be said of his reign?*
    It was as warlike as Numa's reign had been peaceful. His most memorable act was the destruction of Alba Longa.

36. *What was done to the people of Alba Longa?*
    They were taken to Rome and located on the Coelian Hill. The Albans and Romans now became one nation as the Sabines and Romans had in the days of Romulus.
37. *Who succeeded Hostilius?*
    Ancus Marcius, 641 to 616 B. C.
38. *What may be said of his reign?*
    He conquered many Latin cities and brought the inhabitants to Rome, giving them homes on the Aventine Hill.
39. *Who now conquered Rome?*
    The Etruscans.
40. *What were their characteristics?*
    They were builders as well as founders. They adorned Rome with elegant edifices of Etruscan architecture and extended around the city a stone wall which lasted eight centuries.
41. *Whom did they place on the throne?*
    Tarquinius Priscus.
42. *How was his reign distinguished?*
    By great exploits in war and great works in peace.
43. *What improvements did he make?*
    Built the great sewers of the city, many of which still remain. He also planned the Great Race Course (Circus Maximus) and its games.
44. *How did Tarquinius come to his death?*
    Was assassinated by jealous enemies.
45. *Who succeeded him?*
    Servius Tullius, 578 to 534 B. C.
46. *What may be said of his reign?*
    It was very peaceful.
47. *What great thing did he do?*
    Reformed the Constitution and laws.

48. *What other great work did he do?*
Extended the walls of the city until "Rome sat on seven hills."

49. *Name the Seven Hills included in the Servian Wall.*
Palatine, Aventine, Capitoline, Cælian, Quirinal, Viminal and Esquiline.

50. *Who were the two great Classes at Rome?*
The Patricians and Plebeians.

51. *Which was the ruling Class?*
The Patricians.

52. *Who were they?*
The descendants of the first settlers. They were rich, proud and exclusive and demanded all the offices of the government.

53. *Who were the Plebeians?*
The newer families. They were generally poor, forbidden the right of citizenship and not allowed to intermarry with the Patricians.

54. *How did the Patricians treat them?*
The Plebeians were obliged to serve in the army without pay and were thus forced to borrow money of the Patricians. If they failed in their payments they were sold as slaves by their creditors.

55. *Which class did Servius help?*
The Plebeians.

56. *How did he classify the Romans?*
He divided them into five classes, based on property instead of birth, and these into 193 centuries or companies. The people were directed to assemble by centuries either to fight or to vote and to the new centuriate assembly was given the right of selecting the king and enacting the laws.

57. *How did Servius come to his death?*
He was murdered by one of his sons-in-law.

58. *Who succeeded him?*
    His son-in-law and murderer, Lucius Tarquinius Superbus.
59. *What was the character of the reign of Tarquin the Proud?*
    It was very tyrannical. It lasted from 534 to 510 B. C.
60. *What effect did such reigning have on the people?*
    They became very much dissatisfied with kings for rulers.
61. *What was the final result?*
    They threw off the kingly government, and the tyrant Lucius, or Tarquin, as he was called, was forced into exile.
62. *What did Tarquin attempt?*
    To regain the throne by arms.
63. *What did the Romans do in this emergency?*
    They appointed a dictator who should possess absolute power for six months. A great battle was fought at Lake Regillus in which the Romans were victorious and Tarquin gave up his attempt in despair.
64. *What may be said of Rome for the next 150 years?*
    It was a period of civil wars and internal struggles.
65. *What action did the Plebeians take about 494 B. C.?*
    Their condition becoming unbearable, they departed in a body to the Sacred Mount, leaving the city to the Patricians.
66. *How did the Patricians compromise?*
    By cancelling the Plebeian debt and by assenting to the appointment of two magistrates called Tribunes, to be chosen from the ranks of the people.
67. *What power was given the Tribunes?*
    They could annul any law passed by the senate considered injurious to the Plebeians by pronouncing the word "veto," I forbid.
68. *What was the next measure of relief granted the Plebeians?*
    The agrarian laws (from ager, a field).

69. *What did they ordain?*
    That part of the public or conquered lands should be divided among the poorer people.
70. *What change took place next?*
    The Decemvirate was appointed.
71. *What was the Decemvirate?*
    Ten men appointed to have control of the laws.
72. *How long did this last?*
    For two years. Then the senate finding the laws favorable to the Plebeians forced the Decemvirs to resign.
73. *What remained as the result of the Decemviral legislation?*
    The celebrated code of the Twelve Tables. These laws were engraved on blocks of brass or ivory and hung up in the Forum, where all could read them.
74. *What kind of Government followed the Decemvirate?*
    Two Consuls were elected in place of the Decemvirate.
75. *What was the state of the Plebeian power?*
    In spite of great odds, it was continually increasing and by 300 B. C., Rome possessed a democratic government.
76. *What took place 390 B. C.?*
    The Gauls crossed the mountains and started for Rome.
77. *By what other name were the Gauls known?*
    The Celts.
78. *What did they inhabit?*
    Gaul, the British Isles, and Italy north of the Po River.
79. *What did the Gauls do with Rome?*
    Laid the city in ashes.
80. *What spite had the Gauls against Rome?*
    Rome had fought against the Gauls in the Battle of Clusium.
81. *What was the battle-cry of the Gauls?*
    "**On to Rome.**"

82. *What is the tradition of the siege of the Capitol?*
The citadel, being built on a steep and lofty rock, held out for seven months. At one time, the Gauls, having discovered a narrow path up the cliff, had nearly reached the summit in the night, when the sacred geese kept in the temple of Juno began a loud cackling, which awoke the garrison. Marcus Manlius, the Roman commander, aroused by the noise rushed out, saw the peril and dashed the foremost Gaul over the precipice.

83. *How were the Gauls persuaded to leave the city?*
By the Romans paying a large sum of gold.

84. *What did the Romans now do?*
They partially rebuilt the city, but with great irregularity.

85. *Who was the Roman leader at this time?*
Camillus, who led them in several successful attacks against the Gauls.

86. *What was the domestic condition of Rome?*
A great many poor people suffered on account of the expense of rebuilding their homes.

87. *What was the law of Debtor and Creditor?*
Those who could not pay their debts were carried away into bondage.

88. *How was the domestic trouble settled?*
By a revision of the laws the people at last became united and were ready to commence conquering their neighbors.

89. *Whom did they conquer first?*
After three Samnite wars, which occupied half a century with brief intervals, Samnium became a subject ally and Rome was mistress of Central Italy.

90. *What was the next great struggle of Rome?*
The war with Pyrrhus, the King of Epirus, the greatest general of his age. He assisted the Greek colonists in

the southern part of Italy, against whom the Romans had declared war.

91. *What romantic incident is told of one of the battles of this war?*
When Pyrrhus looked upon the Roman dead, all of whom appeared to have fallen in their ranks with their faces turned toward the enemy, he exclaimed, "If I had such soldiers as these, how easily I could conquer the world."

92. *What was the result of this war?*
Pyrrhus was defeated and having lost nearly all of his army returned to Epirus. The Greek colonies, deprived of his help, were subjugated in rapid succession.

93. *What was now the extent of Roman power?*
Rome was now mistress of Peninsular Italy.

94. *Where did Rome now turn her attention?*
To Carthage, the great rival republic, one of the wealthiest cities of the world.

95. *Where was Carthage?*
On the African coast of the Mediterranean.

96. *Where was the first battle field?*
The Island of Sicily, south of Italy.

97. *How long did the first Punic War last?*
Twenty-four years, 264–241 B. C.

98. *What was the result?*
Carthage surrendered Sicily, gave up all prisoners, and paid $4,000,000.

99. *Who was the great Carthaginian General?*
Hamilcar.

100. *How many Punic Wars were fought?*
Three, extending over a period of eighty years. They finally ended 146 B. C.

101. *Who made the invasion of Italy during these wars?*
Hannibal, the son of Hamilcar. He crossed the Alps

ROME. 65

with an army of one hundred thousand men, cutting new roads through the solid rock.

102. *Who was the Roman leader in the Punic Wars?*
Scipio Africanus.

103. *What was the result of these wars?*
Carthage, which had lasted over seven hundred years and numbered seven hundred thousand inhabitants, was utterly wasted and her territory became a Roman Province.

104. *What was the condition of Rome at this time?*
She now owned at least ten foreign dominions, and was mistress of the civilized world.

105. *What was the effect of these conquests?*
Rome was inhabited by a motley population from all lands and the Roman race itself was fast becoming extinct. Patriotism was a forgotten virtue and the soldier fought for plunder and glory. Though the nobles grew very rich, the curse of poverty ate deeper into the state and the moral nature of the nation lost its vigor.

106. *What great danger next threatened Rome?*
The Barbarians had been collecting north of the Alps and were moving south half a million strong. Six different Roman armies tried in vain to stay their advance.

107. *What was the result of their Invasion?*
They were totally defeated by the Romans under Marius and he was hailed as the savior of his country.

108. *What may be said of Rome for the next few years?*
Social and civil wars reigned almost continually.

109. *Who were the leaders in the Civil War?*
Sulla, who stood at the head of the Roman aristocracy and Marius, the chief of the democracy.

110. *What foreign monarch also carried on war with Rome?*
Mithridates, King of Pontus, maintained a struggle with the Romans for twenty-five years.
111. *Who finally defeated him?*
Pompey, who also reduced Syria, Phoenicia and Palestine and in ninety days cleared the Mediterranean of the pirates that infested it.
112. *When was Julius Cæsar born?*
In the year 100 B. C.
113. *What other great men were born about the same time as Cæsar?*
Pompey, 106 B. C. and Cicero the same year.
114. *What may be said of Cicero?*
He was the greatest of Roman Orators.
115. *Who formed a great Conspiracy in Rome about this time?*
Catiline, who was defeated for Consul; a profligate young nobleman, he formed a plot to murder the Consul, fire the city and overthrow the government.
116. *Who delivered a speech against Catiline?*
Cicero. This speech is considered a masterpiece of impassioned rhetoric and is still studied by every Latin scholar.
117. *What became of Catiline?*
He fell in a struggle for his capture, after he had been convicted of treason, in the year 62 B. C.
118. *What was the Triumvirate?*
The chief men of Rome, Pompey, Crassus and Cæsar, formed a league known as the First Triumvirate. By the support of his two powerful confederates, Cæsar obtained the Consulship.
119. *When Cæsar was elected Consul, what did he do?*
Set out to conquer Gaul, carrying the Roman arms into Germany for the first time. He twice invaded Britain, an island until then unknown in Italy except by name.

120. *When did Civil War again break out in Rome, and between whom?*
   In the year 49 B. C., between the friends of Cæsar and those of Pompey. Cæsar at once marched upon Rome and in sixty days was master of Italy.
121. *What was the result?*
   A total defeat of Pompey's army took place on the plain of Pharsalia.
122. *What became of Pompey?*
   He was beheaded in Egypt, where he had taken refuge.
123. *What was the cause of Cæsar's famous dispatch?*
   He marched into Syria and humbled Pharnaces, the son of Mithridates, so quickly that he wrote home, "Veni, vidi, vici!" I came, I saw, I conquered.
124. *Who now became the Great Ruler of Rome?*
   Julius Cæsar. He was created Dictator for ten years and Censor for three, and his statue was placed in the Capitol opposite to that of Jupiter.
125. *What Civil Act did he do?*
   Revised the calendar, and several laws.
126. *What is said of his Government?*
   Order and justice sprang into new life under his administration.
127. *In the meantime what happened?*
   A great conspiracy was formed against his life by a large body of nobles.
128. *Who were some noted ones in the Conspiracy?*
   Brutus and Cassius, the former his most intimate friend.
129. *What was the result of the Conspiracy?*
   Julius Cæsar was assassinated on the 15th of March, 44 B. C., in the Senate.
130. *What reason was given for his assassination?*
   It was said he meditated making himself king, and

Brutus was probably sincere in this belief, but the others seem to have been actuated by feelings of envy rather than of patriotism.

131. *What was Cæsar's character?*
He was the greatest man Rome ever produced. He was not only an able general and a consummate statesman and politician, but a splendid orator, a fine scholar and an elegant writer.

132. *What was his great crime?*
Having acquired power, he did not know how to lay it down, preferring to retain it, although in so doing he destroyed the liberties of his country.

133. *What did he virtually become?*
The first Emperor of the Roman Empire.

134. *Who now ruled affairs in Rome?*
Mark Antony the Consul.

135. *Who made orations against Antony?*
Cicero, who denounced him in fiery orations styled in imitation of Demosthenes, the Philippics.

136. *What became of Cicero?*
He was killed by Antony's friends.

137. *Who was next chosen Consul?*
Octavius, a youth of nineteen, the great-nephew and heir of Cæsar.

138. *What form of Government followed?*
A second Triumvirate was formed between Antony, Octavius and Lepidus.

139. *What did this triumvirate do?*
They met Brutus and Cassius, the leaders of the conspiracy against Cæsar, on the field of Philippi, and a battle was fought in which the latter were defeated.

140. *How was the power apportioned?*
Octavius and Antony divided the empire between them and Lepidus received Africa.

141. *What became of Antony?*
 He was ensnared by Cleopatra of Egypt, gave up Rome, and after being defeated by Octavius in a naval battle at Actium, stabbed himself.

142. *What was the result?*
 Egypt became a Roman province and Cæsar Octavius was the master of the civilized world.

143. *What title did he receive after his return to Italy?*
 Augustus, by which name he is known in history.

144. *When did he die?*
 August 19th, 14 A. D., at the age of seventy-six years. The Senate decreed that divine honors should be given him and temples were erected for his worship. The month of August was named for him.

145. *What was the period of his reign called?*
 This period, from 31 B. C. to 14 A. D., was called the Augustan Age and was one of peace and prosperity.

146. *What did he do for Rome?*
 He beautified Rome so that he could truly boast he found the city brick and left it of marble.

147. *Who was the wickedest Ruler?*
 Nero II. (54 A. D. to 68 A. D.)

148. *What great crimes was he guilty of?*
 The burning of Rome and the murder of his wife and mother.

149. *Why did he burn the city?*
 In order that he might blame the Christians and then have a pretense for their persecution.

150. *What great man is supposed to have been put to death in this persecution?*
 The Apostle Paul, who must have been at Rome at this time.

151. *When was the Roman Empire divided?*
 In 395 A. D., into an Eastern and Western Empire.

152. *How long did they last?*
 The Eastern Empire lasted at Constantinople for one thousand years, but Rome, the capital of the Western Empire, soon passed into the hands of the Barbarians.
153. *How is the fifth century known?*
 As the era of the Great Migrations.
154. *What were they?*
 The different tribes of Europe poured south and west with irresistible fury, seeking new homes in the crumbling Roman Empire.
155. *Who were the three great barbaric leaders?*
 Alaric the Goth, Attila the Hun, and Genseric the Vandal.
156. *What took place 476 A. D.?*
 The fall of the Roman Empire. The scepter, crown and robe of the king were sent by the senate to Constantinople at the command of the German Chief, Odoacer.
157. *What illustrious Latin writers lived in the last century B. C.?*
 Virgil, Horace, Cicero, Livy and Sallust.
158. *How did the Romans regard education?*
 Very highly. As early as 450 B. C., Rome had elementary schools where boys and girls were taught reading, writing, arithmetic and music.
159. *What is said of the Romans as builders?*
 In military roads, bridges, aqueducts and harbors they displayed great genius.
160. *What road leading from Rome is famous for its beauty?*
 The Appian Way. Its foundations were laid by Appius Claudius 312 B. C.
161. *What is said of the Roman bridges and viaducts?*
 They are among the most remarkable monuments of antiquity. The Romans applied the arch to the construction of massive stone bridges, and valleys liable to inundation were spanned by viaducts resting on solid arches.

162. *What other buildings were constructed on a grand scale?*
Triumphal arches, amphitheatres, public baths and tombs.

163. *What are some of the most famous ruins of Rome?*
The Forum, the Arch of Titus, Arch of Constantine, the Colosseum and Baths of Caracalla. The latter contained sixteen hundred rooms adorned with painting and sculpture.

164. *What was the religion of the Romans?*
A worship of the powers of nature, which degenerated into image worship.

165. *What were the principal public ceremonies of their religion?*
Worship at the shrine of Vesta, the goddess of home, and offerings to the Lares and Penates, the household gods.

166. *What were their public festivals?*
The Saturnalia and gladiatorial shows.

167. *What was the Saturnalia?*
A festival occurring in December and lasting seven days, in memory of the free and happy rule of ancient Saturn. It was a time of general mirth and feasting; wars were forgotten, criminals had certain privileges and slaves were permitted to jest with their masters and were waited upon by them at table.

168. *What is said of the Roman Laws?*
In the 6th century A. D. they were condensed into a code which is still the basis of the civil law of Europe.

169. *What period is called the Dark Ages?*
The six centuries following the fall of Rome, 476 A. D.

170. *What change finally took place in the barbaric tribes that settled in Roman territory?*
They were converted to Christianity.

171. *What did this do for Rome?*
 The people who until the overthrow of the empire had been accustomed to depend upon Rome for political guidance continued to look there for spiritual control.
172. *What was the Bishop of Rome acknowledged to be?*
 The head of the Catholic Church throughout Western Europe.
173. *What was the extent of the Papal power during the Middle Ages?*
 It was very great, increasing steadily till it reached its zenith in the 13th century under Innocent III. He claimed to be an earthly king of kings, and the papal thunder rolled over every nation in Europe.
174. *For what is the 15th century noted?*
 For its ecclesiastical councils, to which many monarchs appealed from the decisions of Rome.
175. *What was the result of this tendency to resist papal authority?*
 Rome was forced to confine its political action mainly to Italian affairs.
176. *What Italian cities attained great importance in the Middle Ages?*
 Venice, Florence, Pisa and Genoa.
177. *What was the power of Genoa and Venice?*
 Their trading princes controlled the money of the world and became the first bankers, the Bank of Venice dating from 1711.
178. *What is the Italian Renaissance?*
 A new School of Art, founded at this time, which revived a knowledge of the treasures of Grecian architecture, sculpture, poetry and philosophy.
179. *What great men lived during this period of Florentine history?*
 Michael Angelo, poet, sculptor and painter; the re-

nowned artists, Raphael and Leonardo da Vinci, and the famous reformer Savonarola, afterward burned for heresy.

180. *What was the condition of Italy in the early part of this century?*
It was enslaved and divided by Austrian despotism.

181. *What was the desire of Italian patriots?*
To unite the country under one government.

182. *Who was proclaimed king in 1861?*
Victor Emmanuel. He controlled all Italy except the Austrian province of Venetia and Rome.

183. *When did these two come under his power?*
In 1866, Italy got back Venice and Verona, and in 1870 Rome, and the king moved his court thither from Florence.

184. *Who is the present King of Italy?*
Humbert I., son of Victor Emmanuel, succeeded to the crown on his father's death, 1878.

THE SARACEN EMPIRE.

1. *What marked the 7th century?*
The rise of Mohammed and the spread of the Saracen Empire.

2. *Who was Mohammed?*
An Arabian reformer who taught a new religion.

3. *What was its substance?*
There is but one God and Mohammed is his prophet.

THE SARACEN EMPIRE.

4. *What did he succeed in doing?*
   He subdued the scattered tribes of Arabia, destroyed their idols and united the people in a nation.
5. *What were his successors called?*
   The Caliphs.
6. *What did they conquer?*
   Jerusalem, Egypt and Spain.
7. *What was the extent of the Arab Dominion a century after Mohammed's death?*
   It extended from the Indus to the Pyrenees. No empire of antiquity had such an extent.
8. *How was the Empire divided?*
   Between the Ommiades, descendants of Omar, who reigned at Cordova, and the Abbassides, descendants of the prophet's uncle, who located their capital at Bagdad.
9. *What Caliph has come down to us in fiction?*
   Haroun al Raschid, the hero of the Arabian Nights.
10. *What magnificent Moorish ruins are in Spain?*
    The mosque of Cordova, and the palace of the Alhambra.
11. *What do we know of the learning of the Arabs?*
    When Europe was enveloped in ignorance, the Saracen Empire had colleges to which students resorted from all parts of the world. The Arabs pushed their experiments into almost every line of study.
12. *How long did the Moorish Kingdom last in Spain?*
    Until the year of the discovery of America, when it was destroyed by Ferdinand and Isabella.
13. *What European people are to day Mohammedans?*
    The Turks.
14. *What is the sacred book of the Mohammedans?*
    The Koran.

ENGLAND.

1. *Where is England?*
   West of Europe, separated from the main-land by the English Channel and Strait of Dover.
2. *What does Great Britain include?*
   England, Scotland, and Wales.
3. *Into how many Periods is English History divided?*
   Five.
4. *What are they?*
   The Prehistoric, the Roman, the Saxon, the Norman, and Royal.
5. *How long did the Prehistoric Age last?*
   From antiquity to the Invasion by the Romans under Cæsar, 55 B. C.
6. *What record have we of the aboriginal inhabitants?*
   Only the mounds, with their implements of stone and bronze.
7. *How long did the Roman Period last?*
   From 55 B. C. to 449 A. D.
8. *What did the Romans do for the country?*
   Made improvements, built roads and bridges, and introduced Christianity.
9. *Who ravaged the country during this time?*
   The wild Celts from the north made invasions while the Roman legions were called back to Italy.

10. *Who assisted the Britons in driving out the Romans?*
    The Germans, under two leaders, Hengist and Horsa.
11. *What reward did the Germans get?*
    Tracts of land, and especially the Island of Thanet.
12. *How did the Germans begin to act?*
    As conquerors, rather than friends.
13. *What did they finally do?*
    They established seven kingdoms in different parts of the island, named collectively, the Saxon Heptarchy.
14. *What became of the Britons?*
    They were henceforth called Welsh, and driven to the mountains on the west coast of the island.
15. *What was the name of some of the German Tribes who invaded Briton?*
    Angles, Saxons, and Jutes.
16. *Why was Briton called England?*
    The land of the Angles, or Angeland, modernized into England.
17. *How long did the Saxon Period last?*
    From 449 A. D. to 827 A. D.
18. *What danger now threatened England?*
    The Danes, or Northmen, were coming from the north. In their light boats they ascended the rivers, and landing, seized horses and scoured the country to plunder and slay.
19. *Who partially converted the Saxons to Christianity?*
    St. Augustine and several monks, commissioned by Pope Gregory the Great.
20. *How many Houses governed England during the Norman Period (827 A. D. to 1399 A. D.)?*
    Four.
21. *What were they?*
    Saxon, Danish, Norman, and Plantagenet.

22. *Who was the greatest Saxon King?*
    King Alfred.
23. *What is said of his reign?*
    He expelled the Danes, and restored tranquillity to the country. According to tradition, a gold bracelet could be left hanging by the roadside without anyone daring to touch it.
24. *What great things did he accomplish?*
    He founded the University of Oxford, improved the laws of the kingdom, and established schools for the education of the people.
25. *What did the Danes do a century later?*
    They came in greater numbers than before, and the Danish King Canute (Knut) won the English crown.
26. *Who followed the Danes?*
    The Saxons were restored for twenty-five years.
27. *What battle ended the Saxon rule?*
    The Battle of Hastings.
28. *Who was the Hero of this battle?*
    William, Duke of Normandy, called William the Conqueror.
29. *Where and when was he crowned?*
    At Westminster Abbey, on Christmas, 1066 A. D.
30. *How did the new king treat the English?*
    Kindly, though he favored the Normans in military and official positions.
31. *What may be said of William's life?*
    It was one of constant turmoil from enemies.
32. *What custom did he institute?*
    Ringing the curfew bell in the evening as a signal that the people should extinguish their lamps and fires, either to prevent conflagration or secret assemblies of those who were hostile to the government.

33. *What was one of his most useful acts?*
 Causing the compilation of the Domesday-Book, which was a register of all the estates in the kingdom.
34. *What is said of William as a sportsman?*
 He was a great lover of hunting, and had forests built for that purpose. He laid waste a tract of country extending thirty miles, driving out the inhabitants, demolishing houses, and even churches, but making no compensation for the injury.
35. *Who succeeded him?*
 William II., surnamed Rufus the Red, from the color of his hair.
36. *What great enthusiasm seized the people of the world during the reign of William II.?*
 The first Crusade.
37. *Who was among the leaders in the Crusade?*
 Robert of Normandy, the eldest son of William the Conqueror.
38. *What was the cause of the Crusade?*
 Palestine had been conquered by the Turks, who ill-treated the Christian pilgrims to the holy places.
39. *What effect did this treatment have on the Christian World?*
 All Christendom arose to arms to take the Sepulchre of Christ from the unbelievers.
40. *Were they successful?*
 After a bloody siege of Jerusalem and a terrible massacre of infidels and Jews, they gained possession of the Church of the Holy Sepulchre, and the kingdom of Jerusalem was founded.
41. *How did William II. come to his death?*
 After a reign of thirteen years, he was accidentally shot while hunting in the New Forest (1100). The people viewed this as a just retribution, for when the Conqueror had destroyed the homes of the Saxons, his son miserably perished.

ENGLAND.

42. *What effect did the union of the Saxon and the Norman qualities have upon the English race?*
The blending of the Saxon independence with the Norman skill and learning gave new life and enterprise, a firmer government, and more permanent institutions.

43. *What is said of the power of the Barons?*
It was very great. Their castles became mere robber-nests, and they plundered the common people without mercy.

44. *Who succeeded the Norman Kings?*
The Plantagenets, Henry II., the first of them, becoming king in 1154.

45. *What is meant by Plantagenet?*
Count of Anjou, Henry's father, always wore a sprig in his cap. The sprig was of Genesta, the common broom of Anjou, hence he was nicknamed the "Plantagenet."

46. *Was this name given to his descendants?*
It was, to the whole line, who ruled for 245 years.

47. *What did Henry II. do for law and order?*
He organized an army, destroyed the castles of the tyrannical nobles, and created new barons, who, being English, were ready to make common cause with the nation.

48. *How did he offend his people?*
By his quarrel with Thomas à Becket, Archbishop of Canterbury, caused by his effort to regulate ecclesiastical authority, and make it subservient to civil power.

49. *By whom was Henry succeeded?*
Richard the Lion-hearted.

50. *When did he rule, or wear the crown of England?*
From 1189 A. D. to 1199 A. D.

51. *Who was Richard?*
A Frenchman, a Crusader, a Poet, and a Hero.

52. *What was his character?*
   A hero in the third Crusade; a hater of unbelievers.
53. *Of his ten years' reign, how long was he in England?*
   About one year.
54. *Where did Richard go?*
   Embarked with an army for the Holy Land.
55. *What army joined him?*
   The French, making in all 100,000 men.
56. *What was his success abroad?*
   He conquered the Isle of Cyprus, and the seaport of Acre, and several other cities, but was prevented in his attack on Jerusalem by the dissensions and desertion of his French allies, under King Philip.
57. *What was the result of the pilgrimage?*
   King Richard made a truce with Saladin, Sultan of Egypt, thereby securing several Mediterranean ports, with freedom of pilgrimage to the Christians.
58. *What happened at home during this time?*
   King Philip, who had deserted him, had returned, and was assisting Richard's brother John in the attempt to subdue all Richard's dominions.
59. *What did Richard do on hearing the news?*
   He started for home in haste. He landed on the coast of the Adriatic, and commenced his journey through Europe disguised as a merchant (1192 A. D.).
60. *What happened to him at Vienna?*
   He was recognized by his enemy, the Duke of Austria, and imprisoned. He escaped by paying a large ransom. The English people were forced to give one-fourth of their incomes and even to pawn the church-plate.
61. *On his release what did he do?*
   Returned to England, forgave his enemies, and expelled King Philip from his dominions. He was killed by one of his servants in the year 1199 A. D.

ENGLAND.

62. *Who succeeded King Richard?*
    King John, 1199 A. D. to 1216 A. D.
63. *What was the character of his reign?*
    It was brutal and exacting. He imposed taxes at pleasure, wronged the poor and plundered the rich.
64. *What did this bring about?*
    The whole nation rose in insurrection and the barons with their forces marched against London and took it.
65. *What did they compel the king to do?*
    To grant the famous great charter (Magna Charta) at Runnymede.
66. *What may be said of the Magna Charta?*
    It was the basis of the English Constitution, and as the kings were always trying to break it, they have been compelled, during succeeding reigns, to confirm its provisions thirty-six times.
67. *What was one of the most important articles of the Magna Charta?*
    That no delay should take place in doing justice to every one, and no freeman should be taken or imprisoned, dispossessed of his free tenement, outlawed or banished unless by the legal judgment of his peers.
68. *Who succeeded King John?*
    His son, Henry III. (1216-1272 A. D.)
69. *What is said of Henry's reign?*
    It was noted for civil war. The House of Commons was established, a branch of the English Legislature, which has proved the chief bulwark of the political and civil liberty of the country.
70. *Who succeeded Henry III.?*
    Edward I. (1272-1307 A. D.)
71. *What promise did he make the Welsh?*
    To give them a ruler born in their own land, who could not speak a word of French or English.

72. *Did he keep his promise?*
 He did, in the person of his own son, who was born in their castle the day previous.
73. *To what custom did this give rise?*
 Calling the eldest son of the Sovereign the Prince of Wales.
74. *When did Edward die?*
 In the year 1307, while on an invasion into Scotland.
75. *Who succeeded Edward I.?*
 Edward II. (1307-1327 A. D.)
76. *What Scotch King was his enemy?*
 Robert Bruce.
77. *What battle was fought between them?*
 The Battle of Bannockburn, where 100,000 English were defeated by 30,000 Scots.
78. *When was Scottish independence acknowledged?*
 After 1328. After this, many wars arose between Scotland and England, but Scotland was never in danger of being conquered.
79. *What was the event of the 14th and first half of the 15th century?*
 The hundred years' war with France.
80. *Who succeeded Edward II.?*
 His son, Edward III., aged fourteen (1327-1377 A. D.).
81. *What great battle did Edward III. fight?*
 The Battle of Crecy, against the French.
82. *What did the English use in this battle?*
 Gunpowder, the first they had used in warfare, 1346 A. D.
83. *What was the result of this victory?*
 The capture of Calais. Edward drove out the inhabitants and made it an English settlement.
84. *What did this do for the English?*
 It gave them an open door into the heart of France.

ENGLAND.

85. *Who succeeded Edward III.?*
 Richard of Bordeaux (1377-1399 A. D.).
86. *What was the character of his reign?*
 Continual trouble with French and rebels at home. The first part of his reign is noted for an insurrection of the lower orders of the people, occasioned by the condition of serfdom in which they were kept.
87. *What did King Richard do?*
 He met the people on Smithfield commons, and as their leader had been slain he boldly exclaimed, "I am your king, I will be your leader."
88. *What course did the Parliament take?*
 They refused to ratify the king's pledges, and the insurrection was trodden out by the nobles.
89. *What great reformer lived during this reign?*
 Wickliffe, called by some the "Morning Star of the Reformation." He translated the Bible.
90. *What great poet lived then?*
 Chaucer, styled the Father of English Poetry. He wrote "The Canterbury Tales."
91. *Who succeeded Richard II.?*
 Henry IV., of the House of Lancaster (1399-1413 A. D.).
92. *How long did the House of Lancaster rule, and who were the other kings?*
 Sixty-two years. Henries V. and VI.
93. *What did Henry IV. do?*
 In order to give the discontented nobles war abroad, instead of leaving them to plot treason at home, Henry invaded France.
94. *What was the result?*
 He met a vastly superior French force upon the plain of Agincourt and drove all before him.
95. *What was England's relation to France at this time?*
 England controlled France until the year 1428, when the tide turned.

96. *What great battle or siege occurred in the year 1428?*
 The Siege of Orleans, in France.
97. *Who was the Heroine of this siege?*
 Joan of Arc, a peasant girl.
98. *What did Joan of Arc do?*
 Obtained command of the forces, and drove the English from their fortifications, and saved the city for the French.
99. *What became of the Heroine?*
 She was finally captured by the English, and condemned to be burned to death (1431).
100. *What kind of Sovereign was Henry VI.?*
 Very weak minded, and finally became an imbecile.
101. *What new House of Royalty was rising in England?*
 The House of York.
102. *How long did the House of York rule?*
 Twenty-four years, by Edwards IV., V., and Richard III.
103. *What was commenced in 1455?*
 The "Wars of the Roses," between the Yorks and Lancasters, a struggle concerning the succession to the English throne.
104. *Why so called?*
 The Yorkists wore a white rose and the Lancasters a red one as their symbols.
105. *What was the first battle?*
 That of St. Albans, in which the King was wounded.
106. *How long did this war last?*
 Thirty years; twelve pitched battles were fought and the ancient nobility of England almost annihilated.
107. *Who was the "King-Maker?"*
 The Earl of Warwick, the greatest nobleman of the kingdom. His powerful influence in seating and unseating monarchs won him the title.

ENGLAND. 85

108. *When was Printing introduced into England?*
In the year 1474, by Caxton, of London, the first printed book being, "The Game and Plays of Chesse."

109. *What was the first act of Richard III. when he became king?*
He destroyed the young king, whose throne he had usurped, and his little brother, by an order that they should be smothered in their beds in the tower.

110. *How did he die?*
He was slain on Bosworth Field by Henry Tudor, the last heir of the House of Lancaster.

111. *How long did the House of Tudor reign?*
One hundred and eighteen years.

112. *Who were the Kings of this House?*
Henries VII. and VIII., and Edward VI.

113. *Who were the Queens of the House of Tudor?*
Mary, wife of Philip of Spain, and Elizabeth.

114. *What was Elizabeth called?*
"Good Queen Bess."

115. *What were the characteristic features of this period?*
The rise of Protestantism, the growth of commerce and the development of learning and literature.

116. *What Explorers were sent out by Henry VII.?*
The Cabots, to America.

117. *What was the ruling passion of Henry VII.?*
Avarice. He punished the nobles with fines on every pretext, and resorted to the most unjust and tyrannical exactions.

118. *Who succeeded Henry VII.?*
Henry VIII. (1509-1547 A. D.)

119. *What effect did the crowning of Henry VIII. have on the rival families of York and Lancaster?*
They were united.

120. *How many wives had Henry VIII.?*
Six: Catharine of Aragon, Anne Boleyn, Jane Seymour, Ann of Cleves, Catharine Howard, and Catharine Parr.

121. *What were England's foreign relations at this time?*
    It held the balance of power between Germany and France. Lest either should grow too strong, Henry always took the part of the one who happened at the time to be the weaker.
122. *Who was Henry's minister?*
    Thomas Wolsey, the son of a butcher, who rose from a priest to be Archbishop of York, Lord Chancellor of England, Cardinal and Papal Legate.
123. *What did Henry ask of the Pope?*
    Permission to divorce his wife, Catharine of Aragon, pretending that he had scruples of conscience because she was his brother's widow when he married her.
124. *Did the Pope sanction it?*
    No. He hesitated and the affair dragged on for years, and at last Henry privately married Anne Boleyn, Catharine's Maid of Honor, without papal permission.
125. *How did this step affect Cardinal Wolsey?*
    Because he did not declare a divorce, the king banished him from court. Soon after he was arrested for treason and he died broken-hearted, while on his way to prison.
126. *What was the origin of the English Church?*
    Henry's breach with the Pope. He now denied the Pope's supremacy and Parliament declared the King the supreme head of the English Church. All who refused to take the oath of supremacy were proclaimed guilty of high treason.
127. *What was the character of Henry VIII.?*
    He was, without doubt, one of the most remorseless despots that ever reigned, though he never lost entirely the affection and esteem of his subjects. He persecuted both Protestants and Catholics, the former for rejecting his doctrines, the latter for denying his supremacy.

128. *What translation of the Bible was made?*
   A copy of the Bible was translated by Tyndale and revised by Coverdale, and was ordered to be chained to a pillar or desk in every church.
129. *Who succeeded him?*
   Edward VI. (1547-1553 A. D.)
130. *How old was Edward?*
   He was in his tenth year when he took the reign.
131. *What ecclesiastical changes took place under Edward?*
   The Book of Common Prayer was compiled by Archbishop Cranmer and Bishop Ridley; the Latin mass was abolished and the pictures and statues in the churches destroyed.
132. *What persecution occurred?*
   Many of those who refused to comply with the new liturgy were burned.
133. *Who succeeded Edward VI.?*
   Queen Mary (1553-1558 A. D.).
134. *What did she endeavor to do?*
   Being an ardent Catholic, she sought to reconcile England to the Pope.
135. *What persecution took place?*
   She revived the severe laws against heresy, and one of the most dreadful persecutions on record took place. Nearly three hundred persons were burned at Smithfield, among them being Cranmer and Ridley.
136. *Whom did she marry?*
   Her cousin, Philip II. of Spain.
137. *What name has she borne in history?*
   Bloody Mary.
138. *Who succeeded Mary?*
   Elizabeth ("Good Queen Bess"), daughter of Anne Boleyn, next ascended the throne, 1558 A. D.

139. *What was her character?*
    She had real strength and ability, but she was capricious, jealous, deceitful and vain.
140. *What was the greatest blot upon her reign?*
    The execution of Mary Queen of Scots.
141. *What led to a war with Philip II. of Spain?*
    The people of the Netherlands having revolted against him in consequence of his dreadful oppressions, Elizabeth espoused their cause.
142. *What was the Invincible Armada?*
    The immense fleet that Philip equipped with which to invade England. It consisted of one hundred and forty ships bearing three thousand guns and twenty-seven thousand men.
143. *What was its fate?*
    It was attacked and partly destroyed by a much smaller fleet, and nearly all of the remaining vessels were wrecked off the coast of Scotland.
144. *What may be said of Elizabeth's reign?*
    It was a great literary age.
145. *Name some of the great writers of this time?*
    Shakespeare perfected the drama, Bacon developed a new philosophy, Spenser, Ben Jonson and Marlowe gave form and harmony to poetry.
146. *What family ruled England during the 17th century?*
    The Stuarts.
147. *What was the characteristic feature of this rule?*
    The conflict between the kings bent upon absolute power and the Parliament contending for the rights of the people.
148. *Who succeeded Elizabeth?*
    James I. (1603-1625), son of Mary Queen of Scots.
149. *What is said of his reign?*
    It was an age of voyage and discovery.

ENGLAND.

150. *What Colony did him honor?*
 The colony of Jamestown.
151. *What great war began in his time?*
 The Thirty Years' War (1618 A. D.) in Central Europe.
152. *What was the Gunpowder Plot?*
 The Catholics, disappointed in not receiving the religious liberty they had expected, resolved to blow up Parliament on the day of its opening by the King. Thirty-six barrels of gunpowder were placed in a vault below the House of Lords, and they were to have been fired by Guy Fawkes, a Spanish officer. The plot was discovered on the eve of its execution.
153. *Who succeeded him?*
 Charles I. (1625-1649).
154. *What war broke out during his reign?*
 The Civil Wars.
155. *Who were the contending parties?*
 The King and Parliament.
156. *Who supported the King?*
 The clergy, the nobles, and the gay young men, who disliked the Puritan strictness.
157. *Who supported Parliament?*
 The Puritans, together with London and most of the cities.
158. *What two decisive battles were fought?*
 Marston Moor and Naseby.
159. *What was the result?*
 The King's party was defeated, and he was finally beheaded in the year 1649 A. D.
160. *What kind of Government now ruled?*
 The Commonwealth (1649-1660 A. D.).
161. *Who was the leader of the Commonwealth?*
 Oliver Cromwell.

162. *What was Cromwell's rule?*
 A military despotism. He desired to rule constitutionally, but Parliament proved troublesome and was dissolved. The people were weary of Puritan strictness, and republican and royalist alike plotted against their new tyrant.

163. *What religious body arose at this time?*
 The Friends, or Quakers. They were persecuted for their teachings, and upon the founding of Pennsylvania, many emigrated thither.

164. *Who succeeded Cromwell?*
 His son, Richard.

165. *When was the Kingdom restored?*
 May, 1660 A. D.

166. *Who was proclaimed King?*
 Charles II. (1660–1685 A. D.)

167. *What was he nicknamed?*
 The "Merry Monarch."

168. *What reaction took place?*
 From Puritan austerity, the people rushed to the opposite extreme of frivolity and revelry. The Established Church was restored, and two thousand ministers were expelled from their pulpits as Non-conformists.

169. *What was the year 1665 notable for?*
 The great plague in London. Shops were shut, whole blocks stood empty, and grass grew in the streets. One hundred thousand people died of it in London, and large numbers in other places.

170. *What happened in 1666?*
 A great fire raged for three days, and two hundred thousand people were driven to the open fields, homeless and destitute.

171. *What famous act was passed in 1679?*
 The Habeas Corpus act, which secured all subjects from

imprisonment except where it could be shown to be justified by law. This was designed to check the arbitrary arrests made by the authority of the King.

172. *What famous writers lived during the reign of Charles II.?*
John Milton, the author of "Paradise Lost;" John Bunyan, the author of "Pilgrim's Progress;" Samuel Butler, the author of "Hudibras;" John Locke, the author of "Essay on the Human Understanding;" and the poet Dryden.

173. *Who succeeded Charles II.?*
His brother, James II., Duke of York (1685-1688 A. D.).

174. *What became of James II.?*
By his injustice he was forced to fly to France. His chief aim was to restore Catholicism, and he resorted to illegal measures and persecution to accomplish it.

175. *Who succeeded James II.?*
William and Mary of Orange (1689-1694 A. D.).

176. *How was it accomplished?*
William, Prince of Orange, nephew of King James, and his wife Mary, daughter of the King, and a Protestant, took advantage of the popular indignation and came to England with a large fleet, where they were welcomed by the people.

177. *What important act was passed during their reign?*
The Bill of Rights, which guaranteed the people's liberty, and fixed the government as a constitutional monarchy.

178. *Who was William III.?*
William, by the death of Mary in 1694, became sole ruler, under the title of William III.

179. *What disturbed his reign?*
The plots of the Jacobites, the friends of James.

180. *Who succeeded William?*
Queen Anne (1702-1714 A. D.). "Good Queen Anne," as she was called, was the last of the Stuarts.

181. *When was the union of England and Scotland?*
   In 1707, under the name of Great Britain. It was the chief political event of Queen Anne's reign.
182. *What eminent writers lived at this period?*
   Addison, Steele, Pope, Bolingbroke, and Swift.
183. *When did Anne die?*
   Anne's health was very much affected by the dissensions of her ministers, and she died in 1714, having buried all of her thirteen children.
184. *Who succeeded Anne?*
   King George I., of the House of Brunswick (1714-1727 A. D.).
185. *What does the political history of England under the Georges reveal?*
   An increased power of the House of Commons and a bitter strife between Whigs and Tories.
186. *What did the Whigs favor?*
   The rights of the people.
187. *What did the Tories support?*
   The court and the royal prerogative.
188. *What caused an insurrection in Scotland during the reign of George I.?*
   The attempt of the Jacobites, the friends of the Stuarts, to place the son of James II., called James the Pretender, on the throne. They were defeated, however.
189. *Who succeeded George I.?*
   His son, George II. (1727-1760 A. D.)
190. *What war did the English carry on in America at this time?*
   The French and Indian War, and it culminated in wresting Canada from the French.
191. *What religious body arose during this reign?*
   The Methodists, called so from the zeal and methodic ways of a band of University men who met at Oxford for religious conversation and prayer.

192. *What great leaders belonged to it?*
Whitefield, the preacher; Charles Wesley, the "Sweet Singer;" and John Wesley, the head and organizer of the movement.
193. *Who succeeded George II.?*
His grandson, George III. (1760-1820 A. D.)
194. *What is said of his reign?*
It was the longest of any English King.
195. *What great war occurred in his reign?*
The American Revolution.
196. *What hastened the Revolution?*
The character and unjust acts of the King.
197. *What was the result of the war?*
The independence of the United States, and a war debt for Great Britain of 100,000,000 pounds.
198. *What became of George III.?*
The last ten years of his life he was insane, and finally died in 1820 A. D.
199. *Who followed George III.?*
His son was appointed Regent when his father became insane, and held the office from 1811 to 1820 A. D.
200. *Who succeeded George III. as King?*
George IV. (1820-1830 A. D.)
201. *What is said of him?*
He was styled the First Gentleman of Europe for his courtly manners and exquisite dress, but he was selfish and profligate.
202. *Who succeeded George IV.?*
William IV. (1830-1837 A. D.)
203. *What was he called?*
The Sailor King, from having seen service in the Navy. His warm heart, open hand, and common sense won the love of England.

204. *Who succeeded him?*
   Princess Victoria, daughter of the Duke of Kent, and niece of William IV. (1837 A. D.)
205. *Whom did Victoria marry?*
   Her cousin Albert, of Saxe-Coburg-Gotha.
206. *What has been the character of her reign?*
   Generally peaceable.
207. *Who were the great free traders of England?*
   Richard Cobden and John Bright. They held that every man should be free to buy in the cheapest market and to sell in the dearest without restriction.
208. *What forced a bill abolishing duties upon grain, cattle, etc.?*
   The failure of the potato crop in Ireland and the consequent famine.
209. *Into how many divisions is Parliament divided?*
   Two, the Lords and Commons.
210. *Which House is elected by the people?*
   The House of Commons.
211. *Who assists the Sovereign in ruling?*
   A Cabinet of Ministers or Lords.
212. *If a proposed measure is lost by a vote of Parliament, what is the result?*
   The Ministry resign. The Sovereign then sends for the leader of the opposition, who is requested to form a new Cabinet.
213. *For what is the year 1830 memorable?*
   The opening of the Liverpool and Manchester Railway, upon which passenger cars were drawn by a locomotive engine, the invention of George Stephenson.

FRANCE.

1. *What great empire arose during the Middle Ages?*
   The Frankish Empire.
2. *Who were the Franks?*
   A German race who laid the foundation of France and Germany.
3. *What is the first great event in their history?*
   The conversion of their chieftain Clovis to Christianity because of a victorious battle. Three thousand warriors were baptized with him at Rheims.
4. *Where did he fix his capital?*
   At Paris.
5. *What assisted him in his triumphal course?*
   The power of the Church.
6. *What did he establish?*
   The Merovingian or first Frankish dynasty.
7. *What was the second dynasty called?*
   The Carlovingian.
8. *Who was the great ruler in this dynasty?*
   Charlemagne.
9. *What did he aim to do?*
   To unite the fragments of the Roman Empire.
10. *How did he succeed?*
    After thirty years of war his scepter was acknowledged from the German Ocean to the Adriatic and from the Channel to the Lower Danube. Having restored the Western Empire, he was crowned Emperor at Rome.

11. *What did he next attempt?*
   To organize by law the various peoples he had conquered by the sword. But the work of his life perished with him.
12. *What did his death cause?*
   A division of the Frankish Empire among his children, and this was the beginning of France and Germany.
13. *How was the country named?*
   Lothair's kingdom was called Lotharingia, and a part of it is still called Lorraine. Louis's kingdom was called East Frankland, but the name Deutsch (German) soon came into use. Charles's kingdom was styled West Frankland, Latin Francia, hence France.
14. *What were Charlemagne's characteristics?*
   Keen to detect, apt to understand, profound to grasp, and quick to decide, he impressed all who knew him with a sense of power. He was the best educated man of his age. He mastered Latin, read Greek and some Oriental languages and was learned in astronomy, rhetoric and logic, though he stumbled on the simple art of writing. He was the greatest man since Julius Cæsar.
15. *How did the Norsemen come to settle in France?*
   They ravaged the coast during the days of Charlemagne, and at last one of his successors, Charles the Simple, gave Rollo, the boldest of the Vikings, a province, since known as Normandy.
16. *What change then took place?*
   The Normans, as they were called, adopted the language, religion and customs of the French, and Normandy in time became the fairest province in France.
17. *What was France in the 10th century?*
   A collection of provinces, each with its own government and its own history.

FRANCE.

18. *What was the Feudal System?*
 A king, instead of keeping a standing army, granted a part of his estates or fiefs to his nobles, and they as vassals agreed not only to serve him in person but to furnish upon his call a certain number of armed men ready and equipped for active military service.
19. *When did this flourish?*
 During the Middle Ages.
20. *What dynasty was founded in France in the Middle Ages?*
 The Capetian Dynasty, founded by Hugh Capet, 987. He was the first native French king.
21. *What occurred during the reign of his son and successor Robert?*
 The year 1000 had been predicted as the millennium and this belief occasioned general neglect and idleness. A dreadful famine and pestilence was the result.
22. *How was the power of the Church exercised for the good of the people during the reign of Henry I (1031–1060)?*
 It established what was called the Truce of God, a religious injunction against all military operations from Wednesday at sunset till sunrise on Monday, and on all feast and holy days.
23. *How did it affect the nobles and peasantry?*
 It put a check on the unceasing warfare of the nobles and gave the peasantry an opportunity to cultivate the lands and thus prevent famine and pestilence.
24. *What was an important event in the reign of Philip I. (1060–1108)?*
 Peter the Hermit preached the First Crusade.
25. *Who was Peter the Hermit?*
 A monk who resolved to rescue the Holy Sepulcher in Jerusalem from the Turks.

26. *How did he travel through Italy and France?*
   With bare head and feet, dressed in a coarse robe tied with a cord, bearing a crucifix in his hand and riding an ass.
27. *What did he accomplish?*
   He stirred the people by his appeals and thousands volunteered to follow him. Without order or discipline they crossed Europe, robbing the inhabitants and killing the Jews wherever they went. They all perished either by the way or in the struggle with the Turks.
28. *How many Crusades were there?*
   Eight.
29. *What two military religious orders arose during the First Crusade?*
   The Hospitallers, who wore a white cross on a black mantle, and the Templars, whose badge was a red cross on a white mantle. They vowed obedience, celibacy and poverty, to defend pilgrims, to be first in battle and last in retreat.
30. *How did the Crusades end?*
   In defeat for the Christians.
31. *What was their effect upon Europe?*
   Commerce received a new impulse, the tide of Mohammedan conquest was stayed, and the European states, by coming into contact with the more polished nations of the East, gained refinement and culture.
32. *What was the important event in the reign of Louis VI. (1108-1137)?*
   He gave the towns their first charters, thus relieving large numbers of the lower orders from the condition of serfdom in which they had been kept by the aristocracy.
33. *What were these early municipalities called?*
   Communes or commons (afterward the third estate), and

consisted of citizens leagued together for mutual defense.

34. *What does the history of France during the 13th, 14th and 15th centuries show?*
How she absorbed the great fiefs, one by one; how royalty triumphed over feudalism, and how finally all became absorbed in one great monarchy.

35. *What religious persecution took place in the reign of Philip Augustus (1180-1223)?*
The persecution of the Albigenses, a sect of dissenters from the Church of Rome. Pope Innocent III. preached a crusade against them and their chief defender, Count Raymond of Toulouse. A war ensued, and the most dreadful massacres were perpetrated.

36. *What name has been given Louis IX. (1226-1270)?*
Saint Louis.

37. *What was his reign?*
One of integrity and wisdom, during which France assumed the first rank among European nations.

38. *Who succeeded Louis IX.?*
Philip III., the Hardy (1270-1285).

39. *What terrible event occurred during his reign?*
The Massacre of the Sicilian Vespers.

40. *What led to it?*
He assisted his uncle Charles, King of Sicily, in a war against the Moors. Charles was very odious to the people on account of his arbitrary government and the excesses of his followers, and the result was that on Easter day, 1282, when the church bell sounded for vespers, the Sicilians rushed on all the French they could meet with and massacred 8,000 persons without mercy.

41. *Who succeeded Philip III.?*
Philip IV., called the Fair (1285-1314).

42. *For what is his reign memorable?*
    For the contest he carried on with Pope Boniface VIII. on account of the Pope's attempt to prevent the taxation of the clergy. He treated the Pope's bulls with contempt and after the death of Boniface, he transferred the seat of the papacy from Rome to Avignon, where it remained seventy years.
43. *What did Philip summon for the first time in French history?*
    The States-General or deputies of the Three Estates of the Realm.
44. *What were they?*
    The nobles, the clergy, and the Third Estate or the Commons.
45. *What was the real meaning of this assembly?*
    The French people obtained representation from their King (1302).
46. *How did he treat the Knights Templars?*
    He condemned and abolished this religious and military order which was founded during the Crusades. The Grand Master and many members were burnt to death, while others were treated with shocking cruelty.
47. *What was his motive?*
    The immense wealth of the order excited his greed and jealousy.
48. *What royal house next succeeded to the throne?*
    The House of Valois, in 1328.
49. *Why did this come about?*
    Philip's three sons having come to the throne in succession, died leaving no male heir; and according to the Salic Law no woman could wear the crown.
50. *Why was this called the Salic Law?*
    It was an old law belonging to the barbarous code of the Salian Franks.

51. *Who was the first king of the House of Valois?*
Philip VI.
52. *What other competitor for the throne was there?*
Edward III., of England, the son of the daughter of Philip IV., but his claim was considered invalid by the French through the operation of the Salic Law.
53. *What war was the result of this dispute?*
The Hundred Years' War (1328-1453).
54. *How many kings reigned in France during Edward's reign in England?*
Three; Philip VI., John the Good, and Charles V., during Edward's reign of fifty years.
55. *What was the first great battle of the Hundred-Years' War?*
The Battle of Crécy (1346), in which Philip was defeated.
56. *What was the origin of the title Dauphin?*
Dauphiny was, about this time, annexed to France on condition that the king's eldest son should thereafter bear the title of Dauphin.
57. *What terrible pestilence raged through Europe during Philip's reign?*
The Black Death (1347-1350). It carried off vast multitudes of people, 50,000 in Paris alone. At sea, ships were discovered adrift, their crews having all died; and in Germany, cities and villages were left without a single inhabitant.
58. *Who invaded France during the reign of John the Good?*
The Prince of Wales, called the Black Prince from the color of his armor.
59. *What great battle was fought?*
Battle of Poitiers (1356), in which the French were defeated by a small army of English archers.
60. *What insurrection burst forth at this time?*
An insurrection of the peasantry caused by the misery in which they had been so long kept by the tyrannical nobles.

61. *What is it called in history?*
    The Jacquerie, from Jacques Bonhomme, a name derisively applied to a French peasant.
62. *How did it end?*
    After sacking the feudal castles the peasants were finally defeated in an attack upon one of the towns and massacred by thousands, so that the rural districts were almost depopulated.
63. *Who succeeded Philip VI.?*
    Charles V., surnamed the Wise (1364-1380).
64. *What was the character of his reign?*
    By means of his prudent measures he restored peace and prosperity to the kingdom. The English were deprived of nearly all their possessions in France, and the Royal Library at Paris was founded.
65. *What general commanded the French army at this time?*
    Du Guesclin.
66. *Who succeeded Charles V.?*
    His son, Charles VI., at the age of twelve. His reign coincided with three English kings, Richard II., Henry IV., and Henry V.
67. *How was he afflicted?*
    He was insane for thirty years, and France was, in consequence, a prey to every species of disorder.
68. *Who governed during this period?*
    The Dukes of Burgundy and Orleans. The Burgundians espoused the popular cause and were friendly to England, and the Orleanists, the aristocratic side, and opposed England. Paris ran with blood.
69. *What famous battle was fought with the English?*
    Battle of Agincourt (1415), in which the French were defeated.
70. *Who was the next king of France?*
    Charles VII. (1422-1461.)

71. *Where was he besieged by the English?*
    At Orleans (1428), the last stronghold of his party.
72. *Who was his deliverer?*
    Joan of Arc, a peasant girl, who was impressed with the idea that she was divinely committed to save France.
73. *What did she accomplish?*
    She induced the king and his chief officers to believe in the truth of her mission, and was admitted into Orleans wearing a consecrated sword and bearing a holy banner. Under her leadership the French seemed to be inspired with almost superhuman courage and they compelled the English to raise the siege.
74. *What was she now called?*
    The Maid of Orleans.
75. *What did she urge the king to do?*
    To march to Rheims and be crowned in the great cathedral, which he did after several victorious battles partly under her leadership.
76. *What became of Joan of Arc?*
    She wished to be dismissed, but her services being demanded, she remained in the army. A short time afterward she fell into the hands of the English and was tried and burnt as a witch.
77. *What was the end of the Hundred-Years' War?*
    The English gradually lost all of their French possessions except Calais.
78. *What caused the death of Charles?*
    He was inspired with such terror from the wicked intrigues of his son Louis that he was afraid to take food lest he might be poisoned, and he finally died of starvation.
79. *Who succeeded Charles VII.?*
    Louis XI., sometimes called the Tiberius of France, from his cruelty and superstition.

80. *What epoch does his reign mark in history?*
    The triumph of absolutism. He scrupled at no treachery or deceit to overthrow feudalism and bring all classes in subjection to the crown.

81. *Who was one of the most powerful enemies of the king?*
    Charles the Bold, Duke of Burgundy.

82. *What were his possessions?*
    The Duchy of Burgundy, and nearly the present kingdoms of Belgium and the Netherlands. He held the most splendid court in Europe.

83. *What was the result of their contentions?*
    Charles was defeated in several engagements, and after his death in the last battle, Burgundy was reannexed to the French dominions.

84. *What did Louis wish Mary of Burgundy, the daughter of Charles, to do?*
    As she still retained lands in the Low Countries, the king wished her to marry the Dauphin, his eldest son.

85. *What did she do?*
    She refused her consent and accepted the hand of Maximilian, son of the Emperor of Germany, and Archduke of Austria (1477).

86. *What did this marriage bring about?*
    A rivalry between France and the Empire, which lasted nearly two centuries.

87. *What does the death of Louis mark?*
    The close of the Middle Ages (1483).

88. *Who succeeded Louis XI.?*
    His son, Charles VIII. (1483-1498.) He was only thirteen when he began to reign, and was feeble both in body and mind, and very ignorant.

89. *For what was his reign notable?*
    The invasion of Italy by the French.

90. *What did he attempt to do?*
 To assert the claim of his house to the kingdom of Naples.
91. *What league was formed?*
 The first extended league in modern history was formed by Milan, Venice, the Pope, Germany, and Spain, to expel the invader.
92. *What was the result?*
 After entering Naples in triumph, he retreated and escaped into France.
93. *Who succeeded Charles VIII.?*
 Louis, Duke of Orleans, with the title Louis XII.
94. *What occupied most of his reign?*
 Wars undertaken to acquire possession of territories in Italy.
95. *What heroic Frenchman commanded the army?*
 Chevalier Bayard.
96. *What was the result of the Italian invasion?*
 The French were defeated.
97. *What battle was fought with the English?*
 The Battle of the Spurs.
98. *Why so called?*
 Henry VIII. of England invaded France, and the French cavalry fled very rapidly before him. Chevalier Bayard was taken prisoner in this battle.
99. *Who succeeded Louis XII.?*
 His cousin, Francis I., Duke of Angouleme.
100. *What was his first enterprise?*
 To recover Milan, which he did in the battle of Marignano, totally defeating the Swiss mercenaries.
101. *What treaty did he make with the Swiss Republic?*
 A treaty known as the Perpetual Peace, which lasted as long as the old French Monarchy.
102. *What was now the leading power of Europe?*
 Spain.

103. *Who were candidates for the Imperial Crown?*
   Charles V., of Germany, and Francis I.
104. *What was the result of Charles's success?*
   Francis became his bitter enemy and their rivalry deluged Europe in blood for nearly twenty-five years.
105. *What did both parties seek?*
   The alliance of Henry VIII., of England.
106. *What is said of the meeting of the French and English kings near Calais?*
   Fétes of such extraordinary splendor were given that the place of the interview was called the Field of the Cloth of Gold.
107. *What course was pursued by Henry?*
   Owing to the intrigues of his minister, Cardinal Wolsey, whom Charles had won over, he declared in favor of the Emperor, and they formed a league with the Pope against Francis.
108. *With whom did Francis quarrel?*
   His great general, the Duke of Bourbon, constable of France.
109. *What was the result?*
   Bourbon was taken into the service of the emperor.
110. *What battle was fought in Italy?*
   Battle of Pavia. Having besieged the place, Francis and his army, commanded by an incompetent general, were attacked by the imperialists under Bourbon and terribly defeated.
111. *What happened to the king?*
   He was taken prisoner and carried to Spain, where he remained in captivity for a year, and was only released when he assented to the most humiliating conditions.
112. *What did he do on regaining his liberty?*
   He at once broke his promise and formed an alliance with the Pope, Henry of England, and the Venetians to drive the imperialists out of Italy.

113. *What now followed?*
   The sack of Rome. Charles sent Bourbon into Italy with an army composed partly of adventurers and bandits Bourbon was shot in the first assault, but Rome was taken and for seven months was a scene of violence and pillage. The city never had suffered from Goths and Vandals as now from the subjects of a Christian emperor, the Pope in the meantime being kept a prisoner and treated with the grossest indignities.

114. *With whom did Francis then make an alliance?*
   The Turkish Sultan, Solyman the Magnificent, and many battles followed in Europe and Africa with varying results.

115. *What were the closing scenes of the war?*
   Henry renewed his alliance with Charles and they invaded France from opposite sides. Charles was defeated in a battle, but Henry pushed to within two days' march of Paris, when Francis sued for peace and the treaty of Crespy ended the war of twenty-five years.

116. *Who succeeded Francis I.?*
   His son Henry II.

117. *What form of religion was taking root in France?*
   Protestantism.

118. *What were the Protestants called?*
   Huguenots.

119. *Whom did Henry II. marry?*
   Catharine dé Medici, a descendant of Lorenzo dé Medici, of the Florentine Republic.

120. *How did the King celebrate her coronation?*
   With a bonfire of heretics.

121. *What did the Huguenots claim?*
   Freedom of worship.

122. *What was the result?*
　They were denied, and organized a revolt which plunged France in civil war that lasted during the reigns of Henry's three sons.

123. *Who were the Catholic leaders?*
　Catharine, the Constable Montmorenci and the two Guises, Francis the Duke, and his brother the Cardinal of Lorraine. They were supported by the Church and Spain.

124. *Who were the Huguenot leaders?*
　The King of Navarre, the Prince of Condé, and Coligny, nephew of Montmorenci. They were befriended by the reformers of Germany, England and the Netherlands.

125. *Who succeeded Henry II.?*
　Francis II. (1559-1560), a sickly boy of sixteen, who was ruled by his wife, the fascinating Mary Queen of Scots, and through her by her uncles, the Guises.

126. *What did they attempt to do?*
　To destroy the Huguenots, but after a reign of eighteen months the king died.

127. *Who succeeded him?*
　Charles IX., a child of ten, and Catharine, the queen-mother, as **regent**, tried to hold the balance between the two parties.

128. *What measures were adopted?*
　Leaders of both religious parties were placed in the great offices of state, and entire freedom of religion was proclaimed by the States General and confirmed by a royal edict.

129. *Was this effectual?*
　No. The Catholics, becoming exasperated, resented every concession to the Huguenots, while the Huguenots, growing exultant, often interrupted the worship and broke the images in the Catholic churches.

130. *What was the result?*
A series of eight civil wars, which, interrupted by seven short and unsteady treaties of peace, lasted over thirty years.

131. *What led to the Massacre of St. Bartholomew's Day?*
Coligny and other Protestant leaders gained such an influence over the king that Catharine, seeing her power on the wane, entered into a conspiracy to assassinate them and thus arouse the vengeance of the Huguenots, so that a pretext might be found for their destruction. The plot failed, and she then wrung from the king his consent to the death of Coligny.

132. *What followed?*
The Massacre of St. Bartholomew on August 24, 1572. Before day-break, Catharine gave the signal, and bands of murderers thronged the streets. Coligny was the first victim, and in Paris alone ten thousand persons perished, while in the provinces each city had its own Bartholomew.

133. *What was the result?*
Many moderate Catholics joined the Protestants, and the king died at last a victim of remorse.

134. *Who succeeded Charles IX.?*
Henry III. (1574-1589.) Frivolous and vicious, he met with contempt on every side.

135. *What caused his death?*
Having caused the assassination of the Duke of Guise, the leader of the Catholics, he was stabbed to the heart by a fanatic instigated by Guise's sister.

136. *What ended with him?*
The House of Valois, a house distinguished for misfortunes.

137. *What royal family now came into power?*
The House of Bourbon.

138. *Who was the first Bourbon king?*
 Henry of Navarre, under the title of Henry IV. (1589-1610.)
139. *What battle took place between the Huguenots and Catholics?*
 The famous battle of Ivry, where the Huguenots followed Henry's white plume to a signal victory.
140. *What did he do finally to end the struggle?*
 He abjured Protestantism and declared himself satisfied of the truth of the Catholic faith.
141. *What was the Edict of Nantes?*
 An edict granted by the king in 1598 in which he confirmed the rights and privileges of the Huguenots, conferred upon them entire liberty of conscience and admitted them to all offices of honor and emolument.
142. *What did he do for France?*
 With his famous minister, Sully, he restored the finances, erected public edifices, built ships, encouraged silk manufacture and endowed schools and libraries.
143. *What caused his death?*
 He was assassinated in 1610 in the streets of Paris by a half insane fanatic named Ravaillac.
144. *Who succeeded Henry IV.?*
 His son Louis XIII., at the age of nine years.
145. *Who administered the government during his minority?*
 The queen-mother Maria de Medici. She squandered so much money upon her favorites that Sully resigned his office and went into retirement.
146. *What great man became the chief adviser of the king when he came of age?*
 Cardinal Richelieu.
147. *What did Richelieu determine to accomplish?*
 To destroy the Huguenots as a party, to subdue the nobles, and to humble Austria.

148. *How did he accomplish the first?*
By building a stone mole across the entrance to the harbor of Rochelle and shutting out the English fleet, Richelieu reduced that Huguenot stronghold.

149. *How did he subdue the nobles?*
He destroyed the feudal castles and attracted the nobles to Paris, where they became absorbed in the frivolities of the court, thus weakening their provincial power.

150. *How did he humble Austria?*
By supporting the Protestants during the Thirty-Years' War.

151. *What conspiracies were formed against him?*
Many by the rebellious aristocracy who hated him, but he detected each plot and punished its authors with merciless severity.

152. *What did he do for France?*
He made its power respected by every foreign state. He was also a patron of science and literature, and he founded the French Academy.

153. *Who succeeded Louis XIII.?*
Louis XIV. (1643-1715) at the age of five years.

154. *Who administered the government?*
Anne of Austria, the queen-mother, became regent, and Mazarin, a former disciple of Richelieu, was appointed prime minister.

155. *What was the result of renewed hostilities with Austria?*
Splendid victories were gained by the French army under two renowned generals, Condé and Turenne.

156. *What treaty closed this long war?*
The Treaty of Westphalia, in 1648, by which the boundaries of France were settled nearly as they exist at present.

157. *What took place on the death of Mazarin?*
   Louis assumed the government, and for over fifty years he was sole master in France.
158. *What was his famous saying?*
   "I am the State," by which he claimed absolute right over the life and property of every subject.
159. *What gave him the title of the "Grand Monarch"?*
   The vastness of his military enterprises, the grandeur of his plans for the internal improvement of his kingdom, his magnificent court ceremonial and his patronage of literature, and the arts and sciences.
160. *What impolitic act did Louis commit?*
   By the advice of Madame de Maintenon, whom he married after the death of the queen Maria Theresa, he revoked the Edict of Nantes (1685).
161. *What followed?*
   A fierce persecution of the Huguenots, which drove over two hundred thousand of the best artisans to foreign lands, whither they carried arts and industries hitherto known only to France.
162. *What four great wars did Louis wage to gratify his ambition?*
   War with Flanders, war with Holland, war of the Palatinate, and war of the Spanish Succession.
163. *What effect did these wars have upon France?*
   The country was impoverished, the revenues mortgaged for years in advance and the industries destroyed.
164. *What great palace did Louis XIV. build?*
   Versailles, at an expense of over eighty millions of dollars.
165. *How is the latter part of the 17th century known?*
   As the Age of Louis XIV.
166. *What was the relation of the king to art and literature?*
   Poorly educated himself, being scarcely able to read and

write, much less to spell, he was munificent in his rewards to men of genius. A throng of writers, scientists, poets, and painters clustered about the throne.

167. *Who became king at the death of Louis XIV.?*
His great-grandson Louis XV., at the age of five.

168. *What was the condition of France?*
The public debt was enormous, the government had no credit, and the regent, the Duke of Orleans, was a man without honor or principle.

169. *What followed?*
An era of vice. The world had not seen such a profligate court since the days of the Roman emperors. War added hundreds of millions to the already hopeless debt, and Louis's death left the country plunged in anarchy and ruin.

170. *Who succeeded Louis XV.?*
His grandson, Louis XVI., a good, well meaning young man, but deficient in judgment and decision.

171. *What caused great difficulty at once?*
The irreparable confusion of the finances.

172. *Who was the queen?*
Marie Antoinette, of the hated House of Austria.

173. *What was her character?*
Young and fascinating, she was thoughtless and extravagant.

174. *What was the condition of the lower classes?*
They were overwhelmed by taxation, while the nobility and clergy, who owned two-thirds of the land, were exempt. Men were sent to prison without trial or charges and kept till death. The laws were enacted by those who considered the common people born for the use of the higher class.

175. *What did the strife between classes awaken?*
An intense hatred.

176. *What was the religious thought at this time?*
    Skepticism prevailed, and all that is elevating in religion and morals was made the subject of ridicule.
177. *What did all these conditions develop?*
    The French Revolution.
178. *How did the king try to meet the national difficulties?*
    By choosing ministers of financial skill, among them the celebrated Necker, a banker of Geneva, and finally by assenting to the assembly of the States General, which had not met in a hundred and seventy-five years.
179. *What was the National Assembly?*
    The Third Estate, or Commons, proving to be the most powerful body in the States General, invited the nobles and clergy to join it and declared itself the National Assembly.
180. *What course did the king take?*
    The king and his ministers, dismayed at the determination of the Commons, attempted to exclude them from the hall, whereupon they went to a tennis court nearby and swore not to separate till they had given a constitution to France.
181. *How did the king show his indecision?*
    By sanctioning their measures and requesting the deputies of the clergy and nobility to meet with the Commons.
182. *What led to an insurrection in Paris?*
    Large bodies of troops were collected by the court about Versailles to overawe the assembly, and the Paris mob, excited by this menace to the people's representatives, stormed the Bastile, a noted prison, and razed it to the ground (July 14, 1789).
183. *What did the mob compel the royal family to do?*
    To return to Paris from Versailles, where they were without any support save the Swiss and German mercenaries.

184. *What did the Assembly decree?*
 The entire abolition of the principles and practices of the former government.
185. *What was the Legislative Assembly?*
 The National Assembly, having adopted a constitution, adjourned, and a new body was chosen, called the Legislative Assembly, to which none of the members of the old Assembly were eligible.
186. *What was the character of the Legislative Assembly?*
 Most of its members were ignorant and brutal. The most respectable were the Girondins; the most bitter were the Jacobins.
187. *Who were the leaders of the Jacobins?*
 Robespierre, Danton, and Marat, noted for their wickedness and cruelty.
188. *What further excited the Parisian mob?*
 Austria and Prussia declared war upon France in order to rescue the King.
189. *To what did this lead?*
 The palace of the Tuileries, where the king lived, was sacked by the furious populace, the Swiss guards massacred, and Louis was sent to prison.
190. *What course did the Jacobins now take?*
 They arrested all who opposed their revolutionary projects, condemned and massacred them in the most shocking manner.
191. *What new assembly was organized?*
 The National Convention.
192. *What measures did it take?*
 It formally abolished the monarchy, and declared France a republic, September, 1792.
193. *What was one of its first acts?*
 It tried the king for conspiracy against the liberties of France, condemned him to death, and caused him to

be executed by the guillotine one week later, January 21, 1793.

194. *What was then inaugurated?*
The Reign of Terror, during which thousands were seized and hurried to the guillotine, among them the queen, Marie Antoinette.

195. *What was the fate of the leaders in this?*
Marat was assassinated by Charlotte Corday, a young girl who gave up her life to rid her country of this monster; Danton, showing signs of relenting, was guillotined, and several months later the Reign of Terror ended by the execution of Robespierre himself.

196. *What was the Directory?*
A new constitution was now adopted by the Convention, and the executive authority was intrusted to a Directory consisting of five members.

197. *What brought Napoleon Bonaparte into notice?*
The new constitution was opposed by several of the Parisian Sections (divisions of the city), and an insurrection was threatened. Napoleon Bonaparte, a young officer, was selected to conduct the military operations against the insurgents. He dispersed them, leaving five hundred on the pavement, and the people were subdued.

198. *What command was given Napoleon?*
The command of the Army of Italy, although he was only twenty-six years old.

199. *What did he achieve?*
A succession of brilliant victories over the Austrian armies, which ended in the Treaty of Campo Formio (1797), in which Belgium was ceded to France, and Austria allowed to take Venice.

200. *What expedition did Bonaparte next undertake?*
An expedition to conquer Egypt as a means of attacking the commerce and power of England in the East.

201. *What was the result?*
   He defeated the Turks in several battles, and gained possession of the country, but was defeated himself in a naval battle with the English under Lord Nelson.
202. *What did he find on his return to Paris?*
   Foreign disgrace and domestic anarchy. A coalition had been formed against France by the great powers of Europe, and the Directory had become very unpopular.
203. *How was the change in the government effected?*
   At the point of the bayonet, and a new constitution was adopted, vesting the executive power in three consuls, Bonaparte and two others, elected for ten years.
204. *What military success did Bonaparte win as First Consul?*
   His brilliant victory over the Austrians, at Marengo, restored northern Italy to France. This was followed by a treaty of peace with England.
205. *To what office was he next elected?*
   Consul for life.
206. *What were some of his measures?*
   He restored the Catholic church, he established a uniform system of weights and measures known as the Metric System, he formed the Napoleonic Code of Laws, he repaired old roads, and built new ones, among which was the magnificent route over the Simplon Pass into Italy, even now the wonder of travelers.
207. *What was Bonaparte's next advance?*
   He caused himself to be declared by the legislature, Emperor of the French. The Pope was present at the coronation, but when he lifted the crown Napoleon took it from his hands and placed it on his own head, and afterward crowned Josephine as empress. He subsequently caused himself to be crowned King of Italy.

208. *What did Napoleon do for the next five years?*
   He made war with Prussia, Russia, Austria, and Spain, winning great victories and gaining new territory for France.
209. *Where did he meet the English?*
   In a naval battle off the coast of Cape Trefalgar, where he was defeated.
210. *How did he ally himself with Austria?*
   He divorced Josephine and married Maria Louisa, daughter of the Emperor of Austria.
211. *What did he do in 1812?*
   He invaded Russia with a half-million of men, because the emperor, Alexander, would not accede to his arbitrary demands.
212. *What city did the French enter?*
   Moscow; but the Russians had set it on fire before abandoning it, and the soldiers found no shelter from the approaching winter.
213. *What compelled Napoleon to retreat from Moscow?*
   His soldiers died by thousands of cold and hunger, and as the Czar refused peace, he had no other alternative.
214. *What great officer distinguished himself at this time?*
   Marshal Ney; he was called "Bravest of the Brave."
215. *What did Napoleon do during the retreat from Moscow?*
   He abandoned the army and fled in disguise to Paris.
216. *What was done in 1813?*
   The powers of Europe united in a Sixth Confederation against France, and Napoleon, with a new army, after three victorious battles, was defeated in the "Battle of the Nations," at Leipsic.
217. *What occurred in 1814?*
   The allied powers invaded France, entered Paris, and Napoleon, who had fled from the city, was obliged to abdicate the throne of France and of Italy, and to re-

FRANCE. 119

turn to the island of Elba, which had been assigned him as a residence.

218. *Who was placed on the throne?*
Louis XVIII., brother of Louis XVI.

219. *What happened within a year?*
Napoleon escaped from Elba and hastened toward Paris. He was received with enthusiasm by his troops, and Marshal Ney, who had been sent to oppose his progress, deserted to him.

220. *What did Louis do?*
He fled, and Napoleon found himself again on the throne of France.

221. *What step did the allied powers take?*
They collected three vast armies to oppose Napoleon.

222. *Where was the decisive battle fought?*
At Waterloo, June 18th, 1815, when the army under the Duke of Wellington repulsed the French and drove them into irretrievable retreat and ruin.

223. *What became of Napoleon?*
He fled to Paris, and later surrendered himself to the commander of a British war ship and was carried to England. By agreement of the allied sovereigns, he was sent a captive to the island of St. Helena, where he died six years after, at the age of 52.

224. *What is said of his character and conduct?*
With the talents to have enabled him to confer the greatest blessings on his race, he chose to be its scourge, and sacrificed to his selfish schemes every principle of benevolence and rectitude. During nineteen years of almost constant war, he inflicted upon Europe the most appalling miseries.

225. *What good has come out of his despotism?*
The patriotic efforts demanded to overthrow his power taught the nations of Europe to know their strength.

226. *Where is his tomb?*
   In 1840, his remains were carried to Paris and laid beneath a magnificent mausoleum connected with the Hotel des Invalides.

227. *What measures were adopted by the allies after the battle of Waterloo?*
   They entered Paris, and the greater part of French territory was occupied by foreign armies. Louis XVIII. was restored to the throne, and Marshal Ney shot as a traitor.

228. *Who succeeded Louis at his death?*
   His brother, Charles X. (1824-1830.)

229. *What occurred during his reign?*
   He was bent on restoring Bourbon despotism, and his usurpations led to the revolution of the Three Days of July. The Tuileries was sacked and the king fled.

230. *Who was now elected king?*
   His cousin, Duke of Orleans, received the crown as Louis Philippe (1830-1848).

231. *What was the outcome of his reign?*
   The troubles caused by many conflicting parties, and the King's selfish ambition, culminated in the Revolution of 1848, when Louis Philippe lost heart and fled to England.

232. *What government followed?*
   A republic was proclaimed, and Louis Napoleon, nephew of Napoleon I., was chosen President for four years.

233. *In what way did he become emperor?*
   He plotted by the help of the army a *coup d' état*,—i. e., a stroke of state policy. His opponents were imprisoned, and he was elected President for ten years. Then he obtained the passage of a decree by the Senate, declaring him hereditary Emperor.

234. *What title did he take?*
 Napoleon III.
235. *What did he announce as his policy?*
 "The Empire is Peace."
236. *How did he carry it out?*
 In his reign of eighteen years he engaged in four wars: The Crimean, which brought him great glory; the Italian, the Mexican, and the Franco-Prussian, which caused his downfall.
237. *What was the end of the second empire?*
 The defeat of Napoleon at Sedan, when he surrendered with eighty thousand men. The Empress Eugenie fled to England, and the Emperor died there in exile in 1873.
238. *What did the German army do after Napoleon's defeat?*
 They besieged Paris, which surrendered after four months.
239. *What government followed?*
 The third republic, with Thiers as President.
240. *How was peace purchased by the French?*
 By the cession of Alsace and part of Lorraine, and a penalty of five billion francs.
241. *What was the Commune?*
 In 1871 the Parisian rabble inaugurated a second reign of terror. Another siege of Paris followed more disastrous than the first, and the Tuileries and many of the finest public buildings were destroyed.
242. *What is said of the administration of Thiers?*
 It was singularly successful, and the payment of the war penalty within two years excited the wonder of the world.

GERMANY.

1. *When and how was the empire of Charlemagne divided?*
   After the battle of Fontenay, in which the sons of Charlemagne fought with each other over the vast inheritance left by him, the empire was divided into three portions, France, Germany and Italy, and Germany was assigned to Louis (843).

2. *What happened when the Carlovingian race became extinct?*
   The Diet or Great Council, consisting of the provincial rulers and the dignitaries of the Church, assumed the right of electing the emperor, subject to the Pope's confirmation, by whom alone he could be crowned.

3. *What races occupied Germany?*
   Franks, Saxons, Bavarians and Swabians.

4. *What was the difference between France and Germany in the growth of the monarchy?*
   In France, the crown gradually absorbed the different fiefs and formed one powerful kingdom, while in Germany, the states continued jealous, disunited, and often hostile.

5. *Who were the first rulers of Germany?*
   Conrad, Duke of the Franks; and after a troubled reign he named with singular nobleness Henry of Saxony, his chief enemy, as his successor.

6. *What was the great event of his reign?*
   An irruption of the Magyars or Hungarians, a barbarous tribe. He and his son Otto I. defeated them in two great

battles, and they settled down peaceably, and by the year 1000 became Christian.

7. *What did Henry do to protect the people against their barbarous enemies?*
He founded walled towns and built fortresses, around which villages soon grew up.

8. *How did the burgher class arise from this?*
He ordered every ninth man to live in one of these burghs, as the fortresses were styled, which gave them the name of burgher. They became the great support of the Crown in the disputes with the nobles.

9. *How long did the Saxon dynasty last?*
Through the 10th century.

10. *What ruler of this dynasty was especially notable?*
Otto the Great (936-973). He held the German tribes together and also subdued Italy, being crowned by the Pope, Emperor of the West.

11. *What did this re-establish?*
The Holy Roman Empire.

12. *What effect did this have on Germany?*
While the emperors were absent for years sometimes, protecting their Italian interests, the dukes and counts at home were becoming sovereign princes; and Germany instead of growing into a united nation remained a group of almost independent states.

13. *What dynasty ruled during the 11th century?*
The Franconian dynasty.

14. *What was the notable event of the reign of Henry IV. (1056-1106)?*
His contest with Pope Gregory VII.

15. *Who was Pope Gregory and what was his aim?*
Hildebrand, son of a poor carpenter, monk of Cluny and confidential adviser of five popes. He was resolved to

reform the Church and make it supreme over the civil power.

16. *How was Henry IV. humiliated?*
Resisting the Pope, he was excommunicated, and the German Princes threatened to elect a new king. He sought the forgiveness of the Pope and was forced to stand barefoot on the frosty earth at Canossa three days, before he was allowed to enter the castle and receive the kiss of peace.

17. *What dynasty ruled during the 12th and half of the 13th century.*
The Hohenstaufen dynasty.

18. *Who was the first king?*
Conrad III. of Swabia.

19. *For what is his reign noted?*
For the beginning of the civil wars between the papal and imperial parties, called respectively the Guelphs and Ghibellines. These contests harassed Germany and Italy for nearly three centuries.

20. *Who was the most powerful emperor of the Hohenstaufen dynasty?*
Frederic Barbarossa (Red Beard) (1152-1190).

21. *With whom did he engage in contest?*
With the cities of northern Italy that claimed the rights of republics. Although at first defeated, they subsequently triumphed and the emperor submitted to the demands of the Pope.

22. *What was Frederic obliged to do in order to be crowned emperor?*
To hold the Pope's stirrup.

23. *What was the Great Interregnum?*
The twenty years that succeeded the reign of Conrad IV., the last Hohenstaufen King; German patriotism sank so low that at one time the crown was offered to the highest bidder.

24. *Who was finally chosen king?*
    Count Rudolf, of Hapsburg (1273–1291). He was a brave, noble-hearted man who sought to restore order, punish the robber knights and abolish private wars.
25. *Who were the Electors?*
    The leading princes, who had usurped the right of choosing the king.
26. *What influence did the cities have in the Middle Ages?*
    They formed a powerful restraint upon the feudal lords. As there was perpetual war between the cities and the nobles, the former were compelled to ally themselves for mutual protection.
27. *What was the Hanseatic League?*
    A league of over eighty cities that had its own fleets and armies, and was respected by foreign kings. It attained its highest prosperity in the 14th century.
28. *What Line came into power in the latter half of the 13th century?*
    The Hapsburg or Austrian line.
29. *What was the Golden Bull?*
    A decree issued, 1356, by Charles IV. of the House of Hapsburg, determining the prerogatives and powers of the electors and the mode of election. This made the electors the most powerful persons in the empire and perpetuated the divisions of Germany.
30. *What did Charles IV. found?*
    The first university of Germany, at Prague. It became so famous as soon to number seven thousand students.
31. *What was the Council of Constance?*
    A council called by the Emperor Sigismund to settle the dispute between three different claimants for the papal chair. Eighteen thousand clergymen, including cardinals and bishops, with a vast concourse of learned men, knights, and embassadors from the Christian powers were present.

32. *Who was summoned to appear before it and why?*
   John Huss, rector of the University of Prague, having attacked certain doctrines of the Church.

33. *How was he treated?*
   He came under a safe-conduct from the emperor and was then tried, convicted of heresy and burned at the stake (1415).

34. *What became of his ashes?*
   They were thrown into the Rhine, to prevent his followers from gathering them.

35. *Who shared his fate the next year?*
   Jerome of Prague, his friend and disciple.

36. *To what did this lead?*
   A furious war of sixteen years, in the first part of which the Bohemians or Hussites were led by the famous John Zisca. They defeated the armies of Sigismund in many battles.

37. *How did the Hohenzollern House come into power?*
   Sigismund, being in want of money, sold Brandenburg and its electoral dignity for four hundred thousand gold florins to Frederic, Count of Hohenzollern.

38. *What throne do his descendants occupy to day?*
   The throne of Prussia.

39. *What was the First Diet of Worms?*
   A council summoned by Maximilian (1495). It decreed a Perpetual Peace, abolished the right of private war, and established the Imperial Chamber of Justice.

40. *What was the Aulic Council?*
   A court of appeal from the lower courts in Germany, founded by the Emperor.

41. *What did the reign of Maximilian mark?*
   The end of the Middle Ages. This monarch is known in German history as the "Last of the Knights."

42. *What great religious movement was begun under the reign of Maximilian?*
   The Reformation.
43. *Who was the foremost leader in it?*
   Martin Luther. He preached against the doctrines of the Church of Rome and awakened intense excitement throughout Germany.
44. *Who succeeded Maximilian?*
   His grandson, Charles V., one of the greatest monarchs of ancient or modern times.
45. *How did he treat Luther?*
   He summoned him to answer for heresy at the Diet of Worms (1521), and as Luther would not recant, he was denounced as a heretic, and he and his supporters were put under the ban of the Empire.
46. *Why were the Lutherans called Protestants?*
   When the Catholics passed a decree forbidding any further change in religion, the Lutherans formally *protested* against this action, from which they were called Protestants.
47. *What was the next important event in the history of Germany?*
   The Thirty-Years' War, which was begun in 1618, in Bohemia, on account of the attempt of King Ferdinand to extinguish Protestantism in his dominions.
48. *What was the result of this war?*
   The religious independence of the Protestant states was established; Holland and Switzerland were made free, and the German Empire stripped of its ancient power and splendor. The name German Emperor was henceforth merely an empty title of the Austrian rulers.
49. *What action was taken by the Congress of Vienna after Napoleon's defeat at Waterloo?*
   A German Confederation of thirty-nine states was formed.

A permanent diet was to sit at Frankfort-on-Main, Austria having the presidency.

50. *When was the monarchy re-established?*
In 1848, when Frederic William IV. put himself forward as the leader of the movement for German unity. He was supported by the army and finally a new constitution with a limited suffrage was granted.

51. *What were Prussia and Austria each striving for?*
The leadership in Germany, and it was only settled by a seven weeks' war in 1866, in which Austria was defeated and shut out of Germany.

52. *When was Germany finally united?*
In 1871, when King William was proclaimed Emperor of Germany in the Palace of Versailles, during the siege of Paris.

www.ingramcontent.com/pod-product-compliance
Lightning Source LLC
Chambersburg PA
CBHW022137160426
43197CB00009B/1325